THE KINGS GAMBIT:
Unveiling the Mystery of End Times Evangelism

VIC CALES

CONTENTS

DEDICATION

I FIRST LIKE to dedicate this book to our Lord and Savior Jesus Christ. Obviously, apart from Him, we can do nothing. Prayerfully, the words of this book will be His words to encourage you.

Secondly, I dedicated it to you the readers, because, without you, the Gospel would not be preached, so people would come back to God and live with Him eternally.

Thirdly, with honor, it's almost an overwhelming thought to dedicate this book to those who have prayed for me, mentored me, and inspired me even when they didn't know they were — simply by doing what God called them to do in preaching the Gospel.

I love to give honor where honor is due: to my wife Shelly, and twins Joshua and Rebekah, my true treasures. To all my Family, mentors and kingdom leaders who have prayed for me and inspired me to preach the Gospel and to know the Lord Jesus.

I dedicate extreme gratitude to those who did the actual grass-roots work to make this book possible. For Lucas and Krissy Miles and Nfluence network, Billy Hallowell for all his hard work and research, and all who did great work to bring this project to fruition.

I pray and echo the words of Jesus: that all would believe through our message.

INTRODUCTION

$\sim$

S ELF IS THE *strongest position of power the devil holds over every human.* This unfortunate reality is bursting off the pages of today's magazines, TV screens — and, most certainly, throughout the bowels of social media.

The hyper-focus on "my truth" and "your truth" has had a profound impact on "the Truth," yielding dysfunction and cultural pandemonium.

And, as we'll explore in *The King's Gambit*, time is of the essence.

Yet, while society is reeling and confusion is abounding, we also see glimmers of hope and moments of evangelistic opportunity. From revival to explosions of interest in the Bible among young Americans, hearts and minds are being transformed.

After all, the Gospel does what it always does: cutting through the noise to bring healing. While new ways to do evil will emerge, nothing surprises the Lord and the truth can never truly be squashed. The Holy Spirit changes everything — if we let Him.

See, when a person sacrifices self, it's a gambit — a monumental move — to achieve everlasting victory. Hence, the title of this book speaks to this very matter.

In Chess, a game that requires great strategy, grit, and thoughtfulness, a King's Gambit is an aggressive move at the start of the game where the white player decides to sacrifice a pawn in the second turn in an effort to launch an offensive on the opponent's king.

In the context of evangelism, a person must undoubtedly sacrifice oneself to serve the King and, in turn, make sacrifices to help others discover the importance of doing the same.

The Bible tells us that time is short, meaning we must take spiritual lessons from the strategy and care for players put into the King's Gambit, employ them spiritually, and progress in an effort to save souls.

The hard truth about the Gospel is, in order to become a citizen of King Jesus' kingdom we must repent and turn from the kingdom of hell. Culture sells a very different narrative, encouraging us to follow our own hearts and whims. But God is clear about the consequences.

After all, what does it profit a man to win the whole world and lose his own soul?

A commitment has to be made to one kingdom over the other, as being lukewarm leads us absolutely nowhere, stuck in the muck of indecision, immorality, and ethical ambiguity. Or, to pull from another biblical illustration: saltwater and freshwater don't mix, as James 3:11-13 proclaims. If you drink such a mixture, you will die.

Just the same, we will suffer spiritually — and perish — if we try to live in both worlds.

With so much going on around us today, we must reassess where we are individually and corporately, press the reset button where needed in the Western church, return to the true Gospel of Jesus — and set about making sure others are ready and prepared to hear the Truth.

Christ's message, which is crucial to preach, was clear: repent because the kingdom is near. Sadly, the message we hear today in many churches has been watered down with Woke Christianity and has been reduced to something along the lines of:

> Close your eyes with no one looking and just slip up a hand and invite Jesus to come in and have lunch with you. He'll meet you where you are and there's no need to sacrifice yourself; you just say the prayer and come to church and you're good.

But this isn't Jesus' Gospel. "Come and stay as you are" is a sentiment steeped in Woke Christianity — a doctrine definitively taught by demons. And cultural Christianity simply drives home these faulty mantras, deceiving even the most well-meaning people.

If people fall into these traps, they'll be surprised on judgment day when they learn their fate. Falsely confident, they'll quickly learn their penalty.

"But Lord, O Lord no, I believed in you! There's no way I could spend eternity in hell," they'll say. "I went to church. I even went to a marriage seminar and tried to improve myself. I even prayed and got clean and sober. I listened to sermons and worked on improving myself!"

If they have never died to self and truly lived for Him, though, they'll hear an unfathomable response from God:

> I never knew you. You were always working on yourself because that's who you love the most. You never changed citizenships. You never sacrificed the god of self to receive the power of the Holy Spirit from the God of heaven. You would never repent and change kingdoms. I offered you eternal love and paradise, but you kept your citizenship with the king of self.

What a tragic and terrifying conclusion that is absolutely avoidable if we understand the King's Gambit — if we truly comprehend where we are, where we need to be — and how we reach others. And if we strategically sacrifice ourselves for the sake of others.

One of the things that has opened the door for Woke Christianity and other spiritual crises, is that we have camouflaged the kingdom Gospel by not proclaiming it as clearly as we should.

This is why we need a game plan — a King's Gambit blueprint to help us navigate these issues. In this book, we'll explore our End Times urgency in reaching the lost, what we get wrong about evangelism, and the powerful ways we can — by looking at Christ's example — engage others in seeking the truth.

REBUKING EVIL:
AN EYE-OPENING ACCOUNT

D IEDRA'S HEAD WENT *berserk, her body stiffened, and her eyes rolled to the back of her head. Her hands — just moments before in natural form — suddenly morphed into a claw-like posture, settling into an animalistic, bestial pose.*

This scene might seem like it was ripped from the pages of a horror novel, but it was a very visceral and jarring experience — a possession and deliverance that transformed my life and ministry, refined my perspective, and inevitably led to this very book.

But before we explore the details of Diedra's demonic manifestations and shocking deliverance, perhaps it's best to go back to the beginning of the story.

I first encountered Diedra decades ago when she was a teenager who attended a Bible study at my home. I'll never forget my first meeting and asking her what she believed.

"I believe in Jesus and I believe in angels," she said.

Intrigued and unsure of the depths of her understanding underpinning these statements, I followed up with another question: "Who taught you that?" To my surprise, she quickly responded, "Mother Teresa, when I was at the orphanage in Calcutta."

The unassuming young teen, who had long dark hair, deep brown eyes, and an aura of innocence, then divulged she was from India, where she was orphaned and later adopted by a loving American family.

In addition to her storied past, it was immediately evident Diedra wasn't like most of the other American high school students I had encountered; she was humble, quiet, kind, and very soft-spoken.

The small-framed and introverted girl seemed sweet enough, though I soon learned her spiritual knowledge didn't extend far beyond what she had outlined. She knew Jesus' name and believed in the angels, as she had said, but that was about the extent of it.

Beyond those spiritual breadcrumbs, the rest was static — a blank slate I hoped our Bible studies would help fill. After our brief conversation about Diedra's spiritual chops, she took her seat with the other teens and I dove into Scripture.

At the time, I had no idea this modest teen would forever change our lives and my ministry, as what would soon come and spark a spiritual battle that opened the floodgates of intrigue and advance my own spiritual understanding.

I later learned Diedra started coming to youth group because she was dating one of the Christian boys who regularly took part. Much like a magnet, his attendance attracted her participation, luring her into something she might have otherwise avoided.

Sadly, over time, the relationship between the two grew toxic and sexually immoral, descending into an evasive trap that too often ensnares young people today.

And as many unequally yoked love affairs are prone to do, the relationship came to a painful crescendo when the boy abruptly ended things, leaving Diedra feeling hurt, bitter, and, frankly, *enraged.*

Those emotions soon made their way beyond the former couple's purview and into other arenas: mainly, our youth group.

And while there's never a good time for teen angst, the pint-sized drama began to permeate my ministry at the worst of times. The former couple was slated to attend a summer conference with our youth group at a Christian university.

The annual trip, unfolding during the senior year of high school, meant we were heading on a 1,000-mile trek with 44 kids, church elders, and quite the ragtag crew.

Among them, of course, was Diedra, her now-former boyfriend, and a suitcase full of rage and drama threatening to explode at any moment.

The crumbling of their relationship was flat-out disruptive. Predictably, their newfound disdain for one another sullied the first two days of the conference and distracted everyone from honoring and worshipping the Lord.

Once it became clear the fire wouldn't temper without intervention, I took Diedra and her now ex-boyfriend to a private area to try and talk some sense into them.

"You two need to cut this out. This is going to stop!" was the general tone of the talk.

I warned them they would be sent home if they couldn't get themselves together and handle their affairs in a more appropriate and non-combustible fashion.

But the conversation became shockingly confrontational. My primary focus was on the boy, who was a Christian and should have known better than to ignite a sexual relationship — something it became evident he felt convicted over.

At the end of the conversation, I assumed I had gotten somewhere with the two of them, though that proved a faulty supposition.

Before they left the room, I told them they needed to ask each other's forgiveness for what they had done to one another.

"You're going to apologize to her, and you're going to take ownership of it," I said to the boy, before turning to Diedra. "You're going to apologize to him, and you're going to take ownership for it, because it's both your faults, and you both hurt each other."

It was a simple request — and was initially met with reception.

The boy, clearly sorrowful, said, "Please forgive me." But while he was saddened and sobered by his own actions, Diedra's immediate reaction told a different story.

A Demonic Manifestation

The look on Diedra's face suddenly morphed into a deviant scowl that was an undeniable mixture of eeriness, scorn, disgust, and hatred.

Recognizing the message wasn't quite permeating her heart the way I had hoped, I tried to drive my intent home more pointedly.

"Listen, this is your fault, just as much as him," I told Diedra. "You're going to take ownership of this."

I couldn't have prepared myself for what came next.

Diedra's face became catatonic; she could no longer speak. But that was just the beginning of the strange phenomena. Within moments, her hands took a claw-like form, and her eyes rolled up in the back of her head.

Meanwhile, she began uttering a noise that can most aptly be described as "clucking." Yes, clucking — like a chicken or some sort of farm animal. I had never seen anything like it.

Despite my overall lack of experience with demonic sentiments, I knew right away: *She was completely demonized.*

Considering the abnormality and intensity of this behavior, there was no part of me that thought this was a merely psychological manifestation.

I was a rookie in the demonic realm at that point, but it didn't take a rocket scientist to discern Diedra's reaction was profoundly evil.

"Dude, is she demon-possessed or something?" the boy, who was understandably alarmed by her sudden contortions, blurted out.

I quickly silenced him and realized I needed help — and fast. I promptly told her stunned ex not to tell the others what was unfolding but to promptly run and get some of the other ministry leaders.

As it turns out, there was a man speaking at the conference who had done ministry in South America and Haiti; I knew he had dealt with the demonic, and, needless to say, I needed some serious help!

The boy ran and quickly shuffled our undercover exorcist into the room, along with two pastors, and two elders from my church who were also cops. We figured we'd covertly gather everybody we could, as I had no idea what I was dealing with or what needed to be done.

Another problem added to my confusion: many of the conference leaders were cessationists, contending that the gifts of the Holy Spirit had ceased with the apostles.

Not only would they raise an eyebrow at our claims of the demonic, but they'd likely outright deny what was unfolding, putting us in an untenable situation. But that was only one of the many factors we were up against in those stressful moments.

Keep in mind: Endeavoring to keep Diedra's manifestation quiet at a conference filled with chatty teens was like trying to stuff a Macy's Day Parade float under a bed. Regardless, we gathered our ragtag deliverance team and began trying to help Diedra by tossing ourselves deep into the spiritual abyss to try and free her.

The sights and sounds that followed were absolutely wild.

As one of the cops tried to hold Diedra's arm, the tiny teen seemed to exhibit supernatural strength beyond anything I had seen, exerting a noticeable force that seemed impossible for her size.

The situation was moving so fast that it was hard to think and process, especially considering the foggy and undeveloped theological lenses through which I was looking.

At the time, like many of those at the conference, I embraced the notion that most modern situations like this were psychological in nature. I believed the biblical accounts of demonization but was skeptical of cases unfolding today.

Some of the others in the room surely held the same view — but Diedra's manifestation was rattling those presuppositions in real time, forcing me to consider a new course of thought.

We desperately tried to get her free from the demonic that night but were unsuccessful. While there was some improvement, the teen was still utterly mute, with the clucking continuing to be the only discernible noise coming from her mouth.

Adding insult to injury, all of the women at the conference were too afraid to room with Diedra. But after a seemingly never-ending search, we finally found a girl willing to bunk with her. We needed to guard Diedra and ensure her safety throughout the night, so having someone sit with her was a non-negotiable.

As it turned out, it took two full days to free her from the grips of evil.

The battle was characterized by a plethora of bizarre behaviors and expressions. At moments, she writhed and twisted as if in pain. Other times, her eyes would go berzerk and roll completely into the back of her head.

Meanwhile, our efforts to keep the situation quiet were essentially fruitless.

Teenagers have a penchant for gossip and chatter, and this situation certainly offered the kindling to help word spread like wildfire.

Soon, the higher-ups with the conference caught wind of Diedra's story and started to become concerned. Regardless, we pressed on with the deliverance in hopes of ushering in a healing I now knew was essential.

The morning after the initial manifestation, Diedra came out of her room, still out of control and unable to speak. Like a deer in headlights, we tried to collect ourselves as our understanding of the spiritual realm continued to be upended and challenged.

"How do we cast a demon or demons out of somebody?" I silently questioned, as I listened to the few people at the conference who seemed to understand.

We had people slinging the name of Jesus around and trying to figure out the formulas in a desperate effort to get the girl free.

At one point, we were able to expel a number of demons, as Diedra shook, convulsed, and cried. Progress was being made, but the entire experience left all of us in terror. Regardless of the time it took, we were un-dissuaded, diligently working to help this teen find total freedom.

We fervently prayed and repeatedly shared the Gospel with Diedra as we tried to cast out the remaining demons.

We also needed to confront another challenge in the midst of the chaos: Despite Diedra's years in Bible study with us, she had never accepted Christ—and that was painfully evident. Yet accepting Him would be key to her freedom.

Though we'd kept asking her during the ordeal if she wanted to embrace Jesus, we were initially met with auditory silence due to her muteness. At some point, though, she finally began affirmatively nodding that she did indeed wanted to become a Christian.

Suddenly, she was like a little girl desperately wanting to be rescued from the throes of chaos. There was absolutely no doubt she wanted Jesus as her Savior.

A Miraculous, Prophetic Message

Despite Diedra nodding to accept Jesus and get baptized, one hold was still on her before the deliverance was fully effective: her speech hadn't yet returned.

At one point during the worship service, she abruptly raised her finger, pointed to my Bible, and began to rifle through the text. Still unable to speak, she started pointing out Bible verses.

See, we were expecting to simply free Diedra from demonic strongholds but were stunned as this moment – a prophetic manifestation that transformed my life and ministry – took form.

Diedra pinpointed 21 Scriptures, turning to random pages in the text and specifically running her finger over them, one by one.

The moment was remarkable because Diedra knew virtually nothing about the Bible. And yet, taken in their entirety, these Scriptures she pointed to weaved together a tapestry of eternal truths — a heart-altering narrative that left me stunned.

It's no exaggeration when I say this girl could not have told you where John 3:16 is in the Bible. Yet there she was directing us toward 21 verses, meticulously pointing to every word and using her finger like a Hebrew Torah pointer.

The stunning spectacle was one of the most supernatural things I had ever witnessed.

The first nine verses came from Zechariah, then two from Haggai, and then four from Zephaniah. She bounced back to Zechariah and mixed in at least two Psalms before diving, at one point, into Scriptures in Job.

These are the Scriptures Diedra pointed to, in order:

1. Zechariah 1:14 – I'm very jealous for Jerusalem and Zion
2. Zechariah 2:8 – whoever touches you touches the apple of my eye
3. Zechariah 2:10 – I am coming and will live among you
4. Zechariah 2:13 – God has been roused from his holy dwelling
5. Zechariah 3:3-5 – I will clean Joshua, the high priest of Jerusalem
6. Zechariah 3:10 – there will be peace in Israel

7. Zechariah 4:6 – the Holy Spirit will do this
8. Zechariah 4:10 – the earth will rejoice when God reveals Jesus to Israel
9. Zechariah 5:2-4 – all thieves and liars on the earth will be destroyed
10. Zephaniah 2:4-5 – the nations attacking Israel will be destroyed
11. Zephaniah: 3: 8 – I will pour out my wrath upon the nations
12. Zephaniah 3:15 – there will be no more fear in Israel
13. Zephaniah 3:17-20 – I will restore the honor and fortune of Israel
14. Haggai 2:5-9 – the greatest glory the earth has ever seen is coming
15. Haggai 2:23 – Jesus will rule the government of Israel and all nations
16. Zechariah 1:3-5 – repent and return to Jesus
17. Zechariah 6:1-8 – power will go throughout the earth on Israel
18. Zechariah 8:2 – I'm burning with jealousy for Zion
19. Job 42 – after the suffering will come the greater glory
20. Psalm 37:28-40 – Christians will inherit the earth
21. Psalm 38 – pray for this to happen quickly

Diedra stepped forward after this miraculous moment, openly embraced Christ, and was baptized that very evening. The encounter was undoubtedly moving.

But, as I've already hinted, the experience also cut much deeper into my own heart and ministry, shattering everything I thought I knew about theology, demons, and deliverance.

I simply couldn't shake those 21 Scriptures — the verses Diedra began pinpointing to that fateful day. If I'm honest, the ordeal eventually forced me to realize I was making some profound errors in my ministry, limiting God, and depriving myself and others of the power of the Holy Spirit in Scripture.

I was so stirred by those verses that I kept them in a drawer and have often pulled them out over the years to re-read them, trying to make sense of it all. At first, I made misapplications amid my confusion, asking God why this experience unfolded and what He wanted me to do with the resulting Scriptures.

Did it apply to my church – or my life? What did it all mean? The questions were almost endless. But, as time progressed, I began to notice something: Each verse had something to say about eschatology and the biblical "end game."

This might, at first glance, seem strange — that I collected and have put so much time into analyzing the pinpointing of verses by a teen who had clearly been set free from several demons.

But I believe God gave us a message that day — one intended to push me out of my theological stupor and into a better understanding of His power. The experience proved to me that the gifts, miracles, and healings we see in Scripture haven't ceased.

After all, it was virtually impossible for Diedra to calculate all the Scriptures let alone know where they were or what they meant. And yet the meaning is so intensely important.

As the haze cleared and I was able to see the connections, I began to realize God was delivering a message about the destruction of the enemy — a battle the Lord has already won and that's eventually coming to a place of completion.

I have kept the Scriptures concealed for over 30 years, partially because it took time to understand them, but also because I've had many friends in ministry who would have been quite skeptical of the situation surrounding them.

I have only shown them to a few individuals and have never released them publicly – until now. I believe "for such a time as this'" it is God's time to reveal them. You can study them for yourselves and ask the Holy Spirit to give you revelation about them.

But I firmly believe these Scriptures offer a clear understanding of what's to come; they contain and unpack a mystical revelation about the simplicity of what God has always promised: The return of Jesus will catch us off guard, and, though no one knows the day or hour, it could happen sooner than we expect.

In the words of Christ Himself: *It will come like a thief in the night.*

All around us, it feels like the birth pains are kicking up, with spiritual activity hitting a fever pitch. Stories like Diedra's are increasingly prevalent, but just as evil seems to be dominating facets of culture, we're also seeing God move in profound ways.

As we watch the complexities of mini-revivals and outpourings hit at the same time the world is reeling and immorality is exponentially growing, we must answer questions about the signs of darkness we see — and how much longer such events will persist.

But, beyond that, if we really believe we're marching toward the biblical end of days, we have a much more pressing question to ask: What are we doing to further God's kingdom? And If miracles, signs, and wonders are happening in our world, are we recognizing them for what they are?

And, most importantly, are we diligently working as the clock ticks to bring them into the kingdom of Christ?

Before we answer these questions and further explore how to properly evangelize, let's look at some of the signs of the times that should light a fire in each of our hearts to reach the lost.

THE BIRTH PAINS

⌒

WARS. RUMORS OF *wars. Famines. Earthquakes.* These are just some of the "birth pains" Jesus previewed in Matthew 24 — a glimpse into the issues and happenings that will precede his Second Coming before the "end of the age."

Some might argue that these elements — battles, starvations, earth-shaking phenomena — have always been with us, and such an argument would certainly be valid.

But the pace at which these events, among other dysfunctions, seem to be unfolding should have Christians today thinking deeper about a stunning reality: regardless of when Jesus' Second Coming unfolds, every tick of the clock moves humanity closer to the prophetic crescendo we see culminating in Revelation.

Humanity is, of course, always marching closer toward the end of days. But similar to placards on a highway indicating the miles left to a destination, the birth pains detailed by Jesus in Scripture offer signposts alerting people to the proximity of what's to come.

And these signals tell us the race is speeding up and rounding out to its final stretch.

In the coming chapters, we'll explore some of the pieces of evidence pointing to the idea Christ might return sooner than some believe — a reality that should spark deep within the hearts of every believer an unadulterated passion for reaching the lost with the Gospel.

Later, we'll address what such a quest to share Jesus should look like, but we must first explore what Christ told the disciples about the end of the age and why it's paramount to comprehending and navigating the times in which we live.

What's perhaps most telling about the start of Matthew 24 is how Jesus responds when the disciples ask, "What shall be the sign of thy coming, and of the end of the world?" (Matthew 24:3, KJV).

Christ's warning signs for the end of the age come after He delivers a cautionary message, telling His followers to "take heed that no man deceives you." He explains how some will come saying they are Christ and will deceive people with such antics. It's an especially intriguing caution, considering the current state of affairs in America and across the globe.

Mistruths and confusion are the flavors of the day in a great variety of matters, thus concerns about deceit — especially considering the tattered state of some churches today — is paramount.

When it comes to the "wars and rumors of wars," Jesus told His followers not to be troubled. While these events "must come to pass," He said they are not yet the definitive end of days. In fact, these events and the aforementioned famines, pestilences, and earthquakes are what Jesus calls the "beginning of sorrows" (verse 7).

Among some of the other signs mentioned are betrayal, hatred, and a discernible frigidness in the hearts of man. All of it, again, comes down to a spiritual hoodwinking, with reverence for the glory of God and His truth being replaced by the whims of the self.

The obsession with the self is one of the hallmarks of today's culture, and it's done nothing but confuse and confound the masses. It's part of the deceit we see Christ warn about — diabolical lies that lead nowhere good.

"And many false prophets shall rise, and shall deceive many," Jesus says in verse 11, continuing in verse 12: "And because iniquity shall abound, the love of many shall wax cold."

Today, the waxing of coldness is evident all around us in the hearts and minds of a weary culture buying deep into the toxic lie that the self will satisfy.

But contrary to self-obsession, Christ underscores the importance of deeply rooting the Holy Spirit in oneself. He specifically drives home more sobering warnings in verse 24, proclaiming, "For there shall arise false Christs, and false prophets, and shall shew great signs and wonders; insomuch that, if it were possible, they shall deceive the very elect."

That last line about the deceit of "the elect" is stirring and deeply troubling. It's a message many churches have ignored today as they embrace Woke ideology and place various idols before their love of the Lord.

Tragically, some churches have begun to look more like culture than they do Christ. It's precisely what Jesus warned about it, as He explained these deceptions would be just one of the birth pains exposing the reality that we're moving closer to the "end game."

THE SOLUTION TO THE LIES

Ultimately, we have true hope in Jesus when we die to our selfish desires and eschew man's ideologies that run contrary to God. In this surrender, we learn to hear and obey the voice of the Holy Spirit.

See, the only solution to avoid being immersed in the spiritual quicksand that comes when one embraces mistruths is to do exactly what Jesus calls us to in Matthew 24:13: persist and never give up on the hope we have in Jesus.

"But he that shall endure unto the end, the same shall be saved," Christ proclaims.

There's no mystery here; nothing is being shrouded. Jesus is calling His followers to perseverance and faith, imploring believersto always be ready for what's to come.

But it doesn't end there.

Beyond being on guard and ready, He also delivers another message reminding Christians of the pressing essentiality of spreading the Gospel throughout the world — the focus of this book.

"And this Gospel of the kingdom shall be preached in all the world for a witness unto all nations," Christ says in Matthew 24:14 (KJV). "And then shall the end come."

It's essential to note here that Jesus explains how evangelism and the spread of the Gospel will precede the end times. This reality sometimes gets lost amid end of days speculation and discussion.

It's easy to get so caught up in the birth pains and eschatological events set to come that we miss this vital mark. But we have a clarion and clear call, regardless of what's happening in the culture, to be sharing the Good News with everyone around us.

Just a few chapters later in Matthew 28:16-20, Jesus delivers the Great Commission, providing specific instructions to His disciples — and all future believers — to evangelize.

"Go ye therefore, and teach all nations, baptizing them in the name of the Father, and of the Son, and of the Holy Ghost," Jesus tells the disciples. "Teaching them to observe all things whatsoever I have commanded you: and, lo, I am with you always, even unto the end of the world. Amen."

Notice the instructions here say nothing about fixation on the end of days, nor do they encourage panic. Instead, a steadiness — the same consistency with which Jesus guided His followers in Matthew 24 — persists, with Christ pointing back to the essential nature of evangelism and the spreading of His word to people everywhere.

Famed evangelist Billy Graham explored these very themes[1] in his own global preachings and revivals. "We must warn the nations of the world that they must repent and turn to God while there is yet time," he once said. "We must also proclaim that there is forgiveness and peace in knowing Jesus Christ as Savior and Lord."

On another occasion he added[2], "Only God knows when the alarm will sound, ending the work and ministry of evangelism as we have known it."

These quotes help bring to life the urgency of spreading the Gospel — of getting the message to as many as we can before the inevitable blaring of that alarm.

Christ also prophesies His Second Coming in Matthew 24:30 (KJV), describing the "glory" with which He will come and the power that will come with His arrival.

1 Billy Graham Library, "10 Quotes from Billy Graham on World Evangelism," Billy Graham Library Blog, August 17, 2023, https://billygrahamlibrary.org/blog-10-quotes-from-billy-graham-on-world-evangelism/.
2 Billy Graham Library, "10 Quotes from Billy Graham."

"And then shall appear the sign of the Son of man in heaven: and then shall all the tribes of the earth mourn, and they shall see the Son of man coming in the clouds of heaven with power and great glory," Jesus proclaims.

LIKE THE DAYS OF NOAH

And while we know how the story ends, it can sometimes be difficult to stand in the midst of such a topsy-turvy culture. Yet, while we might sometimes feel stunned, nothing surprises the Lord; Jesus predicted all of this centuries ago.

In addition to some of the birth pains, Christ also tells us His Second Coming will happen at a time similar to what unfolded during the "days of Noah." When we look back at Genesis, we see a tragic explanation of how the culture of Noah's day had devolved into pure sinisterism.

"And God saw that the wickedness of man was great in the earth, and that every imagination of the thoughts of his heart was only evil continually," Genesis 6:5 (KJV) reads, with verse 6 continuing, "And it repented the Lord that he had made man on the earth, and it grieved him at his heart."

The next chapter continues, "And the Lord said, I will destroy man whom I have created from the face of the earth; both man, and beast, and the creeping thing, and the fowls of the air; for it repenteth me that I have made them."

The juxtaposition between this description in Genesis that preceded humanity's destruction and the birth pains mentioned in Matthew is notable. The pre-Ark era was colored by "wickedness" — similar to the aspects of the birth pains we're warned about: betrayal, hatred, and frigidness. And that shouldn't be lost on us.

Jumping back to Jesus' words, we know that He will come like a thief in the night.

"But as the days of Noah were, so shall also the coming of the Son of man be. For as in the days that were before the flood they were eating and drinking, marrying and giving in marriage, until the day that Noah entered into the ark, and knew not until the flood came, and took them all away," Matthew 24:37-39 reads. "So shall also the coming of the Son of man be."

Jesus, of course, also gives some caveats, noting in verse 36 that no man, angels — not even the Son — knows the day or hour of His return. This is a notable inclusion here, as many people have foolishly tried to date set, predict, and proclaim when Jesus will come back.

These efforts aren't only fruitless, but they're spiritually dangerous, threatening to undermine the message Christ delivered.

Remember: we're instructed to be discerning and see the signposts as a reminder we're inching closer to this time. These elements simply shouldn't become our obsession, though.

Over the centuries, some have tragically violated Scripture by making proclamations and predictions about the Rapture and other end-times events, ignoring Jesus' own warnings and words. Only God knows, as we're told, but that hasn't stopped many from trying to take eschatological matters into their own hands.

Finding a balance regarding the end of days is critical. Date-setting is certainly a violation of Scripture, yet understanding the signposts in an appropriate way can illuminate our faith and focus us on the Great Commission.

After all, there's a reason God gave us a roadmap — a blueprint to rely on as we navigate our faith and live out His call to share it with others.

So, let's explore some of the other evidence pointing to the reality that Jesus' return is now closer than ever, why that matters, and how this information can properly inform our own spiritual and evangelistic walks.

THE LIGHT OF THE CHURCH

D ECEPTION, RAGE, HURT, vitriol. The list of chaotic adjectives characterizing today's culture are seemingly endless, as the societal lights continue to dim and darkness increasingly sets in.

And while there's much to lament about the current state of our world, there's also a powerful reality that should encourage and inspire Christians: The light of the true church is becoming easier to see amid increasing societal darkness.

Picture the dimmest of rooms or a winding and wooded area with no street lights. The blackness and uncertain nature of these areas can spark fear, as the pervasive darkness prevents people from fully discerning what's around them.

But imagine, for an instant, that a bright light is suddenly turned on, immediately transforming the room or street from a mysterious and terrifying enigma into a clear and navigable place.

The hidden dangers once lurking in the shadows are now uncovered and illuminated, with the light fully exposing them.

In many ways, this analogy can be applied to the authentic church's power and presence in today's culture, particularly when it comes to society's push into the church and attempts to thwart, water down, and confuse biblical truth.

In the midst of so many confounding events and happenings in the darkness of culture — and even within the Christian realm — the true church is becoming easier to see.

As the days march on, the same confusion Jesus warns us about is becoming more prevalent in some denominations. From the apostate church to Woke Christianity, central truths and biblical focus have been superseded and pushed to the side in favor of a self-centered and vapid theology that favors individual whims over eternal truths.

It's impossible to discuss the shift in Christianity without first looking at the broader devolution unfolding within society.

Ironically, just 1 percent of Americans (yes, you read that correctly), said in 2023 the state of moral values in America is "excellent," with an additional 10 percent saying they are "good." The vast majority — 87 percent — contended the conditions on this front are "only fair" or "poor," according to Gallup[3], a polling firm. Plus, 83 percent said things are "getting worse."

And when you dive into the more specific findings, it's easy to see why we're facing such dire self-assessments. We've abandoned God's laws and replaced them with emotion.

The reason we have the "Woke" counterfeit gospel is because believers have been taught to depend on knowledge like the Pharisees and Sadducees instead of the Holy Spirit's revelation and relationship to guide and direct us.

On one front, the impact of a sex and self-saturated culture can plainly be seen, with a whopping 72 percent of Americans believing sex between an unmarried man and woman is morally permissible; just 27 percent disagree.[4]

Similar proportions unfold when asking about women having babies outside of marriage, with 70 percent of Americans saying this is ethical and 27 percent disagreeing.[5]

This chaos also persists for other issues, with majorities of Americans now standing firmly opposed to the Bible as the Word of God. On the life issue, just over half of Gallup respondents (52 percent) said abortion

---

3 Gallup, "Moral Issues," Gallup News, 2024, https://news.gallup.com/poll/1681/moral-issues.aspx.
4 Gallup, "Moral Issues."
5 Gallup, "Moral Issues."

is moral, with only 41 percent expressing the belief that killing the life of an innocent, unborn child is morally wrong.

Even doctor-assisted suicide is getting the public's endorsement, with 52 percent calling it ethically permissible and 44 percent pushing back.

Larger gaps persist on issues like gay or lesbian relations, with 64 percent expressing moral support and 33 percent refusing to cave on the issue.

There are plenty of other statistics I could dive into, but the point is clear: the majority of contemporary culture is no longer embracing a primarily Judeo-Christian ethic. And while those numbers are notable, even more important is understanding how quickly the sands have shifted.

From 2001 through 2023, Gallup[6] recorded major jumps in immorality. Consider in 2001 how 52 percent embraced sex before marriage as moral, with 45 percent stating in 2002 that having a baby outside of marriage is ethical. Those proportions, just two decades later, stood at 72 and 70, respectively.

Gay relations, as well, jumped[7] from 40 percent to 64 percent over that same time.

A Break Into the Church

While culture isn't the kingdom of Christ, it's impossible to ignore the ways in which it has permeated theological institutions and individual Christians' hearts and minds.

A look at some studies on the church today showcases just how pervasive some of these realities have become. A 2017 study[8] from the Barna Group came to some truth disturbing conclusions, noting "Christians are more aware of (and influenced by) disparate views than ever." The question, of course, is how intense this influence has become.

At the time, Barna found that "only 17 percent of Christians who

---

6 Gallup, "Moral Issues."
7 Gallup, "Moral Issues."
8 Barna Group, "Competing Worldviews Influence Today's Christians," Barna, May 9, 2017, https://www.barna.com/research/competing-worldviews-influence-todays-christians/.

consider their faith important and attend church regularly actually have a biblical worldview."[9]

The alarming nature of this statistic cannot be understated. This means fewer than two-in-10 of the people in the pews who consider themselves devout Christians actually had a worldview comporting with the Gospel.

The study more specifically found that 36 percent of practicing Christians embrace ideas tied to Marxism, with 61 percent agreeing with some ideals found in New Spirituality.

"Almost three in 10 (28 percent) practicing Christians strongly agree that 'all people pray to the same god or spirit, no matter what name they use for that spiritual being,'" Barna reported. "Further, the belief that 'meaning and purpose come from becoming one with all that is' has captured the minds of more than one-quarter of practicing Christians (27 percent)."[10]

And more recent surveys paint an even more alarming picture. Dr. George Barna, director of the Cultural Research Center at Arizona Christian University, released the results of his American Worldview Inventory report in 2023, and to say they were sobering would be an understatement.

Dr. Barna (he founded the aforementioned Barna group, but is no longer affiliated) found that the percentage of U.S. adults with a biblical worldview has plunged to just 4 percent. Adding insult to injury, just 1 percent of Americans between 18 and 29 have a biblical worldview.

As it turns out, COVID-19 had a massive impact on some of these already descending perspectives. Or, at the least, Americans dumbed down their faith and more quickly shifted perspectives during the chaos of the pandemic.

"We found a number of things that changed in terms of their views of truth, their views about God, their own assessment of their spiritual commitment, some of their moral perspectives — even their ideas and their behaviors related to religious activity, personal religious activity going to church, reading the Bible, acknowledging their sins,

9   Barna Group, "Competing Worldviews."
10   Barna Group, "Competing Worldviews."

and asking for forgiveness," Dr. Barna told CBN News. "Those kinds of things all shifted pretty dramatically."[11]

From 2020 to 2023, the declines are notable. The percentage of born-again Christians who believed Jesus was sinless during His time on Earth decreased from 58 percent to 44 percent, and those believing their lives had a God-given calling or purpose dwindled from 88 percent to 46 percent.[12]

God's purposes for humanity are present throughout Scripture, and the reality Jesus is sinless is well-established throughout the New Testament. 1 John 3:5 proclaims "in him is no sin" (KJV) and 1 Peter 2:21-23 (KJV) reads:

> For even hereunto were ye called: because Christ also suffered for us, leaving us an example, that ye should follow his steps: Who did no sin, neither was guile found in his mouth: Who, when he was reviled, reviled not again; when he suffered, he threatened not; but committed himself to him that judgeth righteously.

Though there are many other Scriptures affirming this reality, another verse that drives home Christ's sinless nature is 2 Corinthians 5:21 (KJV), which reads, "For he hath made him to be sin for us, who knew no sin; that we might be made the righteousness of God in him."

Christ's perfection is a centerpiece of the Christian faith, making any such departure a truly diabolical development — one that speaks to the problematic nature of the apostate church and its ever-constant move away from biblical inerrancy.

There are other troubling areas where born-again Christians have expressed some unfortunate shifts in recent years.

The notion that human life is sacred — another truth we see in the biblical narrative — has also decreased among this group from 60 percent in 2020 to 48 percent in 2023.

---

11 Billy Hallowell, "God, Truth, Sin, and Church: Shocking Study Reveals How Americans' Shifting Views Are Sparking Biblical Worldview Crisis," Faithwire, May 18, 2023, https://www.faithwire.com/2023/05/18/god-truth-sin-and-church-shocking-study-reveals-how-americans-shifting-views-are-sparking-biblical-worldview-crisis/.
12 Hallowell, "God, Truth, Sin, and Church."

It's tough to find this surprising in a culture overemphasizing the self and undermining the eternal; God's plan for humanity becomes of lesser importance to a people uninterested in anything outside of their own perspective and experience.

This is further reflected in reactions among Christians to a very basic theological statement: "God is the basis of all truth," a proclamation that plunged from 69 percent expressing belief in this sentiment in 2020 to 63 percent saying the same in 2023, according to Dr. Barna.[13]

A COLLECTIVE CONFUSION

All of these findings point to an erosion of Christian values among those who claim to espouse the faith. It's not difficult to see how culture's shifts have invaded every facet of society, including portions of the church.

And yet we know what Scripture tells us about being on guard and craving true wisdom. The Bible makes no bones about the fact humans are prone to following selfish whims, clinging to sin, and finding ourselves drifting away from the truth.

The Apostle Paul implores believers in 1 Corinthians 16:13-14 (KJV) to "stand fast in the faith" and "be strong," urging Christians to stand by truth and do everything "with charity." And Proverbs again and again drives home the essentiality of wisdom.

"The fear of the Lord is the beginning of knowledge," Proverbs 1:7 (KJV) reads. "But fools despise wisdom and instruction." And if there's any confusion about the source of truth, Proverbs 2:6 (KJV) makes its origins more than clear: "For the Lord giveth wisdom: out of his mouth cometh knowledge and understanding."

Sadly, folly has so pervaded many hearts and minds that the fear of God has been usurped by the quest for the self, with the wisdom and love of God being pushed to the wayside. The most telling portion of this verse, though, focuses on reverence for the Lord — a respect so

---

13 Billy Hallowell, "'Shocking' Shift Among Born-Again Christians on Jesus' Sinless Nature: Pastors Would Be Wise to 'Rebuild the Spiritual Foundation,'" Faithwire, April 24, 2023, https://www.faithwire.com/2023/04/24/shocking-shift-among-born-again-christians-on-jesus-sinless-nature-pastors-would-be-wise-to-re-build-the-spiritual-foundation/.

profound it should reorient our hearts to vertical love and worship above all else.

Other verses in Proverbs point to similar calls to embrace such wisdom, revealing how clinging to God's standards will lead to true fulfillment.

"He that getteth wisdom loveth his own soul," Proverbs 19:8 (KJV) continues. "He that keepeth understanding shall find good."

Unfortunately, some truly toxic elements unfold when the cultural megaphone intensifies so much that we decide to let down our spiritual guards, embracing the blaring, counter-biblical messages being spewed rather than the Scriptural truths we're promised will lead to fulfillment.

Proverbs 3:5-6 promises us the Lord will direct our paths and make them straight when we trust in Him and lean not on our own understanding. Yet it's sadly been too easy for some to ignore these Scriptures and to willingly wind through a thorn-filled path of confusion.

Some of this is rooted in complacency, though some is also steeped in a deeper spiritual problem — something embedded in the end of days deceit Jesus spoke about during His earthly ministry.

Many people and institutions today have somehow developed more reverence and fear of the culture than they have for the Lord. It's the very thing Christ warned about in Matthew 10:28 (KJV) when He said, "And fear not them which kill the body, but are not able to kill the soul: but rather fear him which is able to destroy both soul and body in hell."

The failure to live out this warning can be seen today in multiple Christian bodies and denominations as Wokism and confusion plague these institutions. Rather than being Gospel-driven and wisdom-led, these organizations and churches have found themselves suddenly debating issues and realities God has already settled.

MARRIAGE & GENDER

Marriage and gender have been at the forefront of these battles, with some churches and denominations facing splintering and separation when some within question God's design for individuals and families.

The clear narrative presented in Scripture — one man and one woman having a sexual relationship within marriage — has been upended by a confounded culture. And the fixed nature of God's design for the individual to be either male or female has, for some, morphed into a discombobulated quest to bend to every proclaimed pronoun.

These are, of course, just two of the many issues in which fear of culture has trumped reverence for the Lord, though they're perhaps the most prevalent.

As an example, consider the Methodist Church in Great Britain, which released an "Inclusive Language Guide" encouraging believers within its ranks to stop using basic terms deemed too gendered.

"Sharing your own pronouns helps to create a safe space for people to be themselves," the document reads, in part. "In an online meeting, some people share their pronouns after their name: For example: Gemma Hyde, She/her OR Jay Walker, They/them. You could also share your own pronouns in conversation. However, nobody should feel under pressure to do so."[14]

The treatise goes on to document a plethora of other issues related to this conversation, but you get the drift: many today are simply bending to culture rather than relying on the truth, and, in addition to greenlighting deceit, they're wasting quite a bit of time doing so.[15]

On the same-sex marriage front, Christian denominations are finding themselves in complete upheaval, with many departing from Scripture to embark on new definitions of matrimony.

The Anglican Communion and the United Methodist Church are just two denominations in chaos over LGBTQ issues, with the Catholic Church's decision to offer more leeway for the blessings of same-sex couples also ruffling feathers.

As for the Anglicans, furor ignited at the end of 2023 when the Church of England began allowing blessings for same-sex partnerships, though gay marriages remain banned. Regardless, the shift created

---

14 Methodist Church in Britain, ILG Designed Update, December 2023, archived January 17, 2024, accessed February 9, 2025, https://web.archive.org/web/20240117111250/https://www.methodist.org.uk/media/31380/ilg-de-signed-update-december-2023.pdf.
15 Methodist Church in Britain, ILG Designed Update.

consternation among those within the Anglican ranks who firmly disagree with the decision to offer blessings of any sort.[16]

But, as The Associated Press and other media outlets have extensively noted, it is the implosion of the United Methodist Church that stands out among these many disputes, with more than 7,650 churches leaving the denomination.[17]

According to the AP, most of these houses of worship are "conservative-leaning congregations responding to what they see as a failure to enforce bans on same-sex marriage and the ordaining of openly LGBTQ people."[18]

And these splinterings are show no signs of calming down.

A LIGHT IN DARKNESS

Certainly, a number of other issues persist, including pervasive beliefs about universalism and the idea that, contrary to biblical teaching about heaven and hell, everyone will somehow ultimately inherit salvation.

None of this should surprise us, though. Unscriptural views like this will unsurprisingly take root as people and institutions begin to fear man more than the Lord.

All of this disorder and departure from biblical truth can easily lead to anxiety and frustration about what's unfolding, but none of it takes God by surprise.

As we close this chapter, there's an essential takeaway to which we must return: the light of the church becomes increasingly easier to see as the darkness sets in.

Universalism, under which everyone goes to heaven, ordaining homosexual marriage, gender change, and the cultural interpretation seeking to amend the word of God or reject it as the inspired word of God will not be accepted by the true church — and this will undoubtedly upset confused folks.

---

16 Nicole Winfield, "Christian Denominations Are Divided on Blessing Same-Sex Unions. Here's Where They Stand," Associated Press News, December 24, 2023, https://apnews.com/article/lgbtq-samesex-unions-christianity-catholic-anglican-methodist-00e3a4adaf4266dabbf730390eebd2d9.
17 Winfield, "Christian Denominations on Same-Sex Unions."
18 Winfield, "Christian Denominations on Same-Sex Unions."

In the end, though, the rejection of these dysfunctions are making it easier for people to see true Christianity, be attracted to Jesus, and reject man-made and self-focused religion.

Perhaps that's why we're seeing dual movements unfold. At the same time, we have mass confusion, poor theology, and chaos in and outside of the church, we also have sweeping pockets of revival and spiritual awakening — a dynamic we'll further explore in the next chapter.

Reverberations of Revival

—

"*I'VE NEVER SEEN anything like it.*"

That's how evangelist Nick Hall described the stunning spiritual events dominating 2023. As that year came to a close, Hall, founder of Pulse, a global Christian movement training up young leaders to share the Gospel, told CBN News he was certain something deeply spiritual — and different — was truly afoot.

"I think we're in the middle of ... a reformation of sorts," he told the outlet. "I think there's a shift happening. ... A lot of the things that we've put our hope in for a long time aren't working, and I think God is using that to draw many, many people to Himself."[19]

This might seem counterintuitive in a culture immersed in much of the chaos we discussed throughout the last chapter — and, in particular, in a nation in which the population's Christian identity has plummeted from 78 percent in 2007 to 63 percent by the early 2020s.[20]

"As recently as the early 1990s, about 90 percent of U.S. adults

---

19 Billy Hallowell, "'There Is Revival': Evangelist Has 'Never Seen Anything' Like Spiritual Reformation Sweeping America," Faithwire, January 5, 2024, https://www.faithwire.com/2024/01/05/thereis-revival-evangelist-has-never-seen-anything-like-spiritual-reformation-sweeping-america/.

20 Pew Research Center, "How U.S. Religious Composition Has Changed in Recent Decades," Pew Research Center: Religion & Public Life, September 13, 2022, https://www.pewresearch.org/religion/2022/09/13/how-u-s-religious-composition-has-changed-in-recent-decades/.

identified as Christians," the Pew Research Center stated in a 2022 report.[21]

Boy have times changed. But, despite the spiritual devolutions and moral denigration, Hall is on to something.

I'm a firm believer that, spiritually speaking, we're going to see dual dynamics increasingly play out. As the birth pains ramp up and dysfunction rages throughout culture, so will revival.

Of course, this term often carries different connotations and is subject to debate, particularly after the stunning events we saw at Asbury University on February 8, 2023.

A regular Wednesday morning chapel service at the Christian school turned into a nonstop praise and worship service that extended 24 hours a day for weeks, concluding on February 24, 2023.

Asbury has officially called the event an "outpouring," though many saw it as a stunning sign of revival. College students openly embraced Jesus, and people from around the globe flooded to the small town of Wilmore, Kentucky, where the school is located, to take part.[22]

"News of the continuous services spread around the world, and attracted people to Wilmore from as far away as Russia and Japan," an Asbury University explainer detailed[23]. "Media outlets arrived en masse to cover the spiritual awakening among young people. Countless reports of life change, salvation, and re-dedications to Christ were some of the amazing results of the Outpouring events."

It was truly a sight to see — but it wasn't the first time the school experienced the spirit of revival. See, Asbury has a history of such outpourings and revival moments, as do other institutions.

But this event, for many reasons, seemed different from past revivals. Seeing the crumbling moral state of America juxtaposed against pockets of young people suddenly dying to self and clinging to Jesus was quite remarkable.

Many Christians began to feel something extraordinary was afoot — a spiritual awakening igniting a portion of youth who have for too

---

21 Pew Research Center, "U.S. Religious Composition."
22 Asbury University, "Outpouring," Asbury University, 2023, https://www.asbury.edu/outpouring/.
23 Asbury University, "Outpouring."

long been swept up into the lies and deception that have tragically enveloped society.

The stories that emerged from Asbury were quite remarkable. A student at the school named Alexandra Presta spoke out during the outpouring, telling CBN News about the incredible events she personally watched unfold.

"The Holy Spirit chose to just fall down and touch our hearts," she said. "This is purely God moving and keeping people here and bringing more [who are] continuing to cross state lines and even across the country now; it's absolutely insane."[24]

At the same time, other colleges began experiencing similar spiritual outpourings. Lee University in Cleveland, Tennessee, was another place where spiritual fervor seemed to be breaking out around the same time, with Asbury's flames spreading.

Actor and filmmaker Alex Kendrick ("War Room," "Overcomer," and "Fireproof," among many additional projects) visited Lee University during the revival and recounted the powerful sights and sounds he experienced.

"I noticed no one was orchestrating anything. No one was upfront with any agenda," he said. "You had a variety of people sharing quick testimonies, reading Scripture from various points in the room. Someone would stand up and start reading a Psalm or a passage from one of the Gospels, and everyone would agree."[25]

Kendrick said music would then randomly begin, with worship songs abounding.

"It was just a sweet move of God," he said.[26]

And that latter quote really does seem to capture the entirety of what we're continuing to experience right now — a move of the Lord.

---

24 Billy Hallowell, "'Our Culture's Going to Be Changed': Massive Revival at Asbury University Captivates World, Shows No Signs of Slowing Down," Faithwire, February 14, 2023, https://www.faithwire.com/2023/02/14/our-cultures-going-to-be-changed-massive-revival-at-asbury-university-captivates-world-shows-no-signs-of-slowing-down/.
25 Billy Hallowell, "'A Sweet Move of God': Actor and Filmmaker Alex Kendrick Sees Power of Revival Firsthand at Lee University, Praises Experience," Faithwire, February 27, 2023, https://www.faithwire.com/2023/02/27/a-sweet-move-of-god-actor-and-filmmaker-alex-kendrick-sees-power-of-revival-firsthand-at-lee-university-praises-experience/.
26 Hallowell, "'A Sweet Move of God.'"

Asbury and Lee Universities were just small pieces of the overarching puzzle, as churches across the U.S. are recording record numbers of baptisms, among other powerful moves.

DEFINING REVIVAL, REFORMATION, AND RENAISSANCE

Before we continue, it's probably wise to define what revival really means, as the descriptions and definitions are essentially all over the map. Kenneth Berding, a professor of New Testament at Talbot School of Theology, calls Christian revival a "moment in history" comprised of three main facets.[27]

First, he said the "hearts of many of God's people are awakened to greater love and commitment to Christ." Beyond that, Berding said it's a timeframe during which people who might call themselves Christians — but who are actually not — "get converted."[28]

And the final factor is that people who have never known Jesus are gathered to the faith by seeing how the Lord is working in the hearts of His followers.

But, I want to pull back a bit to present my own framing. Revival is a dead-raising term. When something dead comes to life, *that's revival.* Just consider: When a human flatlines, you try to raise the person back up by shocking his or her heart.

Spiritually speaking, revival is the same concept — an important and essential reality of our faith that must be understood.

Of course, Christian revival often seems weird or strange to the secular mind or the immature positioning of some Christians, but the Bible makes its prevalence and importance clear.

Human beings are dead in our sins, but when a person gets saved, they are born again. Revival always comes with conversions. But we can also pinpoint revival as unfolding when we have dead faith that is very literally brought back from the precipice of "death."

Keep in mind: the Holy Spirit "shocked" humanity on the day of

27 Biola University, "What Is Christian Revival? Three Resources to Help You Understand Revival," Good Book Blog, March 2, 2023, https://www.biola.edu/blogs/good-book-blog/2023/what-is-christian-revival-three-resources-to-help-you-understand-revival.
28 Biola University, "What Is Christian Revival?"

Pentecost with tongues of fire and what appeared to be drunkenness, but was, in fact, miraculous tongues bestowed upon believers by the Lord.

Too many forget this reality in the church today, though many believers are in need of revival, specifically those who reject certain core tenets of Scripture.

For instance, a cessationist — someone who rejects the gifts — has dead faith in biblical gifts of the Holy Spirit. But if and when the Holy Spirit opens his or her eyes and dead faith gets born again, these people might change their minds and choose to believe in the gifts.

This is just one form of revival for Christians. Another are believers who have fallen into the trap of nominal Christianity, going through action steps with no heart.

Again, anything that is dead and comes back to life is a revival.

In the context of corporate worship, a dead church can come back to life as well, with believers collectively abandoning apathy for true faith, embracing Jesus' command to love God and love others to the fullest.

Even a person's physical healing can be a form of revival. When the dead limbs of a cripple come back to life and they're suddenly able to pick up their mat and walk, this, too, qualifies. Thus, we see revival at the individual and corporate levels in various forms.

That brings us to another term we must tackle: reformation. It's another stage of what people universally call revival. Martin Luther reformed all of church culture with the *95 Theses* posted on the door of Castle Church in Wittenberg, Germany.

We are saved by grace not by works and he reformed the Catholic Church by driving home that fact. The church is still being reformed today with different denominations and houses of worship emerging and growing.

There are mega churches, storefront churches, churches in business offices, and house churches. We use a lot of different names for these structures, but, regardless of the terminology or structure, we see an undeniable reality: reformation is taking place.

The traditional style of church in America is changing — and that's a good thing. Questions are being asked like:

- What does it take, biblically, to be a church?
- Can you plant an aboveground church in places like Iran, North Korea, Afghanistan or China?
- Why is Christianity thriving in these kinds of places?
- Why are there more miracles signs and wonders in these kinds of churches?
- Why are there fewer lukewarm Christians where there is persecution?
- Why are there more Christians who are willing to die for their faith there?

What's perhaps most remarkable about houses of worship in some of these tough areas of the world is that their churches are not what we consider "traditional" or typical. In fact, they're nothing like what you'd see in the United States.

These churches are many times underground, worshipping in hiding, and meeting needs in secret. Unlike the massive U.S. churches we have where brick and mortar sometimes bring people together to worship in apathy and comfort, these churches cling to truth as they persist through incredible challenges to worship the Lord — sometimes at the risk of their safety or life.

In places like China where the Communist Party controls religion and churches — and is even reportedly creating its own diabolical, inaccurate version of the Bible — we see people launching secretive underground churches.

It's "untraditional" and yet incredibly biblical. See, traditon and comfort can only take you so far; without substance, it all means nothing. Chinese Christians know the government is watering down and hampering the Gospel, so they're willing to risk it all to buck the norm and create illegal house churches.

They know eternity matters and they're willing to honor the Lord with all they have.

Tragically, when comfort or tradition are elevated over truth, dead faith is the end result. We see this today with Wokeness overtaking some churches in America — and beyond.

But, even in in the U.S., where comfort can sometimes trump truth and sow spiritual insanity, we're observing church reformation. People are increasingly leaving Woke churches and abandoning lukewarm pastors to form house churches.

We are beginning to see what I believe could be an underground church reformation throughout the United States — and there's no telling where it could go next.

The next term we'll explore is renaissance. Within the context of the church, renaissance refers to flourishing creativity and new ministries that are being born within Christian circles and houses of worship.

As we've seen throughout history, these new expressions of the Gospel come in its many forms and facets. The term renaissance references new aspects of heaven coming to Earth and emerging through fresh forms of music, theater, dance, technology, beauty that we have never seen before — all efforts that express the kingdom of Christ.

This cyclical process ebbs and flows as time progresses, with bursts of creativity often flowing during difficult or complex times. Today, we're watching Christian films and music take on new forms, cutting through the cultural noise to have a profound Gospel impact.

Thus, revival, reformation, and renaissance are the three phases of true kingdom revival.

LOOKING TO THE PAST

We can discuss and debate the terminology surrounding revival all day long, but, regardless of where people fall, there's no doubt the Lord is fast at work even in the midst of cultural chaos.

In fact, we've seen such spiritual fervor in the past rise up during difficult and harrowing moments.

Stephen Seamands, professor of Christian doctrine at Asbury Theological Seminary, has detailed some past revivals and spiritual moments that have profoundly impacted the world, noting that the Second Great Awakening in the 1800s "produced the abolition movement, which led to a civil war, but [also] social change."[29]

---

29 Michael Foust, "Asbury Prof: 'Outpouring,' Not 'Revival,' Is Best Label for Recent Events," Crosswalk, February 28, 2023, https://www.crosswalk.com/headlines/contributors/michael-foust/asbury-prof-outpouring-not-revival-is-best-label-for-recent-events.html.

The Second Great Awakening ran from around 1795 through 1835 and was comprised of meetings in small towns and big cities throughout America, with church membership growing. Encyclopedia Britannica credits the move of God during that time with sparking the "emancipation of women" and the founding of seminaries and colleges.[30]

This, of course, came after the First Great Awakening, which unfolded from around 1720 to the 1740s. During this time prior to the nation's inception, faith swept through the American colonies. The moment of spiritual renewal came as the Enlightenment — an era that ushered in critique of traditional biblical truth — was overtaking the world.[31]

With religion being subjugated and church attendance decreasing in the process, History notes that some Christians became disillusioned "with how wealth and rationalism were dominating culture."[32]

In many ways, the parallels between culture during the First Great Awakening and today are quite stunning[33]. In the 1700s, many became disenchanted with the newfound quest to accumulate things and started looking back to faith.

As a result, some people returned to church. Preachers like British phenom George Whitefield and revialist Jonathan Edwards swept through the colonies drawing massive hordes of people intent on hearing the inspiring, Gospel message.

And the implications were big both spiritually — and culturally. Some Christians started questioning racial divides and slavery, counting the latter as sinful. Summarizing the extent of the impact, the Bill of

---

30 Encyclopaedia Britannica, "Second Great Awakening," Britannica, 2024, https://www.britannica.com/topic/Second-Great-Awakening.

31 Encyclopaedia Britannica, "Great Awakening," Britannica, 2024, https://www.britannica.com/event/Great-Awakening.

32 History.com Editors, "Great Awakening," History, A&E Television Networks, last modified October 10, 2019, https://www.history.com/topics/european-history/great-awakening.

33 Christianity.com Editors, "The Great Awakening," Christianity.com, Salem Web Network, accessed February 9, 2025, https://www.christianity.com/church/church-history/timeline/1701-1800/the-great-awakening-11630212.html.

Rights Institute noted that the "religious landscape of the new nation was never the same."[34]

That's a pretty bold and telling claim, but one that makes perfect sense upon deeper reflection.

It's no secret the Gospel changes individual hearts, but it's impact, in turn, on the collective whole is sometimes overlooked, especially when such large groups of people are hearing the message — and responding. The Bill of Rights Institute explains just how deep and lasting the impact of the First Great Awakening was on American culture:

> The Great Awakening helped prepare the colonies for the American Revolution. Its ethos strengthened the appeal of the ideals of liberty, and its ministers and the members of the new evangelical faiths strongly supported the Revolution. The drive for religious liberty against a tyrannical religious authority fed into the movement for civil liberty against the unjust political authority of the British in the 1770s. Likewise, the evangelical teaching that each individual believer was equal before God made it easier for people to accept the radical implications of democracy and to question authority.[35]

Today, the issues are different but the situation is equally ripe for God to transform lives in a revival or massive spiritual sweeping of similar magnitude. Tragically, people today have been inundated with a self-centered way of living — the so-called "gospel of the self."

But, while this contagion has captured many hearts, there appear to be cracks in secularists' arguments. Just as the colonists found themselves disillusioned by the materialistic trappings of the world, people today are increasingly waking up to the fact they've been swept up in a lie — and they've begun turning back to God for answers.

And that's an incredible phenomenon to watch. It's one we also saw in the 1970s when a beleaguered generation started finding Jesus again in droves.

---

34 Bill of Rights Institute, "The Great Awakening," Bill of Rights Institute, accessed February 9, 2025, https://billofrightsinstitute.org/essays/the-great-awakening.
35 Bill of Rights Institute, "The Great Awakening."

Known as the Jesus Movement, it was a time of profound disarray in America when young hippies rebelling against the status quo found faith. Greg Laurie, pastor of Harvest Christian Fellowship in Riverside, California, and leader of the Harvest Crusades, became a Christian during that time and has had a massive impact ever since.

In many ways, it feels like we're in a similar situation once again.

It's possible to argue the Asbury outpouring and other related events were a fluke, though a fair look at all the factors seems to expose God being at work in the hearts and minds of many across America today.

A Deeper Movement of God

Without a doubt, the spiritual fervor throughout 2023 and 2024 was off the charts. It seemed to start in early January when Buffalo Bills safety Damar Hamlin cardiac arrested and collapsed on the field and the entirety of the NFL, sports media — heck, even the nation at large, openly turned to prayer.

Then, the release of *Jesus Revolution*, a film telling the story surrounding Laurie and the Jesus Movement rocked the box office just as the Asbury outpouring was dominating headlines internationally.

And the spiritual events didn't halt there. Just weeks later, Baptize SoCal, an effort from faith leaders in California, saw 4,166 people get baptized at the historic Pirate's Cove (where thousands of baptisms happened during the 1970s Jesus Movement).[36]

That historic number of baptisms was then almost immediately shattered when Laurie held another baptism and saw 4,500 people immersed in just one day — potentially the largest ever recorded in American, if not world, history.[37]

The energy behind these moments hasn't waned either, as many churches continue to report historic numbers of baptisms and increased interest in the Gospel.

Again: As culture continues its moral descent, something seems

---

36 Billy Hallowell, "85-Year-Old Man Whose Family Thought He'd Never Find Jesus Gets Baptized at Greg Laurie's Historic Event: 'Never Give Up on People,'" Faithwire, July 12, 2023, https://www.faithwire.com/2023/07/12/85-year-old-man-whose-family-thought-hed-never-find-jesus-gets-baptized-at-greg-lauries-historic-event-never-give-up-on-people/.
37 Hallowell, "85-Year-Old Man Gets Baptized."

to be simultaneously happening to awaken the hearts of Americans, particularly young people.

Some might be confused by this dynamic, wondering how revival or spiritual resurgence could unfold as ethics implode and End-Times prophecy points toward increased chaos.

Such a question is important to address, and preachers like Laurie have done so. While he admits "there's a lot going on in our world right now,"[38] Laurie was also quoted by CBN News in 2022 explaining his views on the nature of revivals.

"The reality is: revivals often happen during times of crisis," he said. "We need one, and I think the very backdrop of our culture reminds us of that, and it might be the perfect moment for it to happen again."[39]

The point is: the world can — and will — be heading in the dire direction the Bible has prophesied, but that doesn't mean pockets of revival and turning back toward God can't and won't happen.

In fact, people will still be turning to the Lord even as the End Times clock inches toward a close. If anything, the uptick in revival-like moments is even more of a reason to urgently pray and reach others with the Gospel.

We could fill the pages of many books with the signs that point us toward the notion the end could be approaching sooner than many believe.

While we've only scratched the surface here, the exploration thus far has left us with an important reality: the chaos and encouragement unfolding around us should ignite a quest in our hearts to share Christ with the lost.

But how do we do that in a sound, biblical, and compelling way? What steps do we take? Next, we'll now ponder the importance of evangelism in the midst of such uncertainty. We'll start by exploring some of our evangelistic errors, and why they matter.

---

38 Billy Hallowell, "Can Another Great Awakening Unfold if End-Times Prophecy Says Things Will Worsen? Greg Laurie on Why a 'Jesus Revolution' Is Possible," Faithwire, March 3, 2023, https://www.faithwire.com/2023/03/03/can-another-great-awakening-unfold-if-end-times-prophecy-says-things-will-worsen-greg-laurie-on-why-a-jesus-revolution-is-possible/.
39 Billy Hallowell, "Are the End Times Upon Us? Greg Laurie Breaks Down Why Understanding Bible Prophecy Is So Essential," Faithwire, March 8, 2022, https://www.faithwire.com/2022/03/08/are-the-end-times-upon-us-greg-laurie-breaks-down-why-understanding-bible-prophecy-is-so-essential/.

WHAT CHRISTIANS GET WRONG ABOUT EVANGELISM

Now THAT WE'VE established that the signs of the times are pointing us toward an ever-approaching end of days, we must recognize the next logical reality: if we believe the end is near or, at least drawing closer, our passion must be increasingly ignited to bring the Gospel to every man, woman, and child.

This naturally brings us to the main purpose of this book: *evangelism*.

In an increasingly complex culture, it's easy to lose the focus and willpower to openly and robustly share Christ's love with friends, loved ones, and strangers.

From apathy to ignorance and even fear over retribution, there's no shortage of self-imposed barriers impeding Christians from living out the Great Commission. But don't just take my word for it; a series of surveys and polls show the depths of the problem.

The Barna Group exposed in a 2018 survey how little Christians reported sharing their faith, with the polling firm noting at the time "growing number of Christians don't see sharing the good news as a personal responsibility."[40]

In 1993, the polling organization found that nine in 10 Christians

---

40 Barna Group, "Sharing Faith Is Increasingly Optional for Christians," Barna, May 15, 2018, https://www.barna.com/research/sharing-faith-increasingly-optional-christians/.

agreed with the proclamation "Every Christian has a responsibility to share their faith," but this dropped to just 64 percent by 2018.[41] Somehow, Jesus' call to "go into all the world and preach the Gospel to all creation" has become an optional quest for far too many professing believers.[42]

Some of us spend eons discussing and debating over the "how" and "why" behind this spiritual disaster, though we do have some statistical breadcrumbs that can help us get closer to an understanding of what's driving the lack of evangelistic understanding and activity.

A separate 2022 Lifeway Research survey actually yielded some encouraging numbers. As it turns out, 93 percent of Christians are at least somewhat willing to have a conversation with a friend about faith, and 81 percent said the same about speaking with strangers.[43]

But the heartening statistics seem to halt there, as 52 percent said they believe encouraging people to change religious ideals is "offensive and disrespectful." An even larger percentage — 66 perent — aren't familiar with methods through which they can tell others about Jesus.[44]

And a more recent 2023 study from the Barna Group further probed this issue, finding that 52 percent of Christians who attend a church at least monthly and say faith is important in their lives see an implicit responsibility to share their beliefs with others.[45]

Yes, you read that correctly — that's just a little over half of these self-professed believers find it important to do what they're called to do.

And there you have it: many Christians don't seem to feel equipped, don't understand how to evangelize, or don't fully understand their biblical calling.

---

41 Barna Group, "Sharing Faith Is Increasingly Optional."
42 Bible Gateway, "Mark 16:15, New International Version," Bible Gateway, accessed February 9, 2025, https://www.biblegateway.com/passage/?search=Mark%2016%3A15&version=NIV.
43 Lifeway Research, Evangelism Explosion: Survey of American Christians Report, August 4, 2022, https://research.lifeway.com/wp-content/uploads/2022/08/Evangelism-Explosion-Survey-of-American-Christians-Report-8_4_22.pdf.
44 Nicole Alcindor Kyriacou, "Two-Thirds of Christians Don't Know Methods for Sharing Jesus: Study," The Christian Post, August 9, 2022, https://www.christianpost.com/news/two-thirds-of-christians-dont-know-methods-for-sharing-jesus.html.
45 Barna Group, "Why Christians Don't Share Their Faith," Barna, Aug. 16, 2023, https://www.barna.com/research/christians-share-faith/.

Considering evangelism is a command that comes directly from Christ, this complacency feels not only ignorant but also spiritually dangerous.

While the statistics clearly show some calling themselves Christians don't necessarily feel a responsibility to share, the bigger issue is that believers feel ill-equipped. Hiding in the shadows and declining to approach friends, family, and strangers with the Gospel message becomes the easier approach — a journey of least resistance, if you will.

And it's not just those sitting in the pews. Even pastors report not doing the best job reaching non-believers with the Gospel, with just two in five[46] preachers telling the Barna Group they feel they're effective at reaching this population or even inviting those who don't embrace Christianity to their churches.

This passiveness is undoubtedly having a negative impact, as a heart-breakingly low percentage of unchurched Americans — just 29 percent — report that a Christian has ever shared with them in a one-on-one conversation how to become a believer; just 35 percent report hearing about the benefits of the Christian life, according to Lifeway.[47]

Just let that reality set in for a moment. Many believers are evading their biblical mandate.

There's plenty more we could say about this dynamic, and we'll get into the nitty gritty. But we can summarize the multifaceted details as follows: there's much Christians get wrong about evangelism, with these pervasive issues impacting even those who are actively engaging in the practice.

In the following chapters, we'll explore these conundrums in detail, looking at the specific pitfalls, what's driving these barriers — and how Christians can persist to properly and effectively sharing the truth.

---

46 Barna Group, "Why Christians Don't Share Their Faith."
47 Aaron Earls, "Christians Don't Share Faith with Unchurched Friends," Lifeway Research, September 9, 2021, https://research.lifeway.com/2021/09/09/christians-dont-share-faith-with-unchurched-friends/.

MISUNDERSTANDING THE
BELONG-BELIEVE-BEHAVE MODEL

ONE OF THE most prevalent errors made on the evangelism front today pertains to a tragic misunderstanding surrounding something known as the "belong, believe, behave" model.

What is this, you ask? Well, when Jesus first encountered sinners, He allowed them to *belong* without changing His message. And yet many people today demand conformity before understanding, bending without willful pliability — and transformation without spiritual comprehension.

Like somehow expecting a toddler to have a viable command of complex physics or algebraic equations, we demand people conform and reform without being taught — or experiencing — how such complex reformations unfold.

But, as we discuss this dynamic, there are two realities with which we must contend. First and foremost, the Holy Spirit can swiftly move to bring instantaneous understanding to a person and dramatically change them in an instant.

Though some people's spiritual understanding takes more time, the Spirit can immediately transform someone.

And secondly, we cannot make the grave error of going the wavering way of Wokism, acting as though "belonging" and "staying as you are" are part of Jesus' final plan for mankind.

See, Christ is the prototype of what — and how — we are supposed to be; He's our example and North Star. He lived and behaved a certain way and He expects us to do the same, reflecting His being and character in our own lives.

Jesus didn't just talk the talk; He displayed the walk. And it's a walk we're all called to embrace as we seek to live out our faith in a healthy and vibrant way.

"Verily, verily, I say unto you, he that believeth on me, the works that I do shall he do also," Jesus proclaimed in John 14:12 (KJV). "And greater works than these shall he do; because I go unto my Father."

Comprehending this verse's meaning is necessary to understanding the truth behind the "belong, believe, behave" model and to recognizing more broadly what we too often get wrong about evangelism.

The Great Commission is a powerful calling from Jesus, but He didn't give us one commission when He told His disciples in Matthew 28:18 to "go and make disciples of all nations, baptizing them in the name of the Father and of the Son and of the Holy Spirit" (NIV).

Christ also gave authority to believers in Matthew 10 to heal the sick, raise the dead, cast out demons, and preach the kingdom.

And Jesus also proclaims in Acts 1:8 that the Holy Spirit will grant the disciples power — spiritual abilities that would make them "witnesses [for Christ] in Jerusalem, and in all Judaea, and in Samaria, and unto the uttermost part of the earth" (KJV).

The best way to understand how Jesus spoke to sinners is to simply observe the biblical text. Christ spoke with prostitutes, tax collectors, and sinners, often offending the religious. He offered His love and the option to belong, but didn't bend or compromise His message in the process.

In turn, belief and faith were planted and incubated in individuals' hearts, allowing many of them to give their lives to Him in repentance. It was then that the Holy Spirit was ready to be received, to work in men's hearts, and for their behaviors to finally change.

Sadly, some in the church today have taken a different route, attempting in a proverbial sense to "clean fish before they catch them."

Just as there are many baits in the tackle box of a fisherman, there are various types of evangelism, with each type's deployment depending on the circumstances, needs, and types of "fish."

When we fail to understand there are various approaches and we decide to share the Gospel without respect or context, we cannot expect to see fruitful results.

Furthermore, if we simply refuse to understand the proper order through which we're called to engage, the end result will similarly fail to "catch" anyone for the kingdom.

The Messiah came to pursue His bride and His demeanor was one of the most powerful baits in His tacklebox. His kindness and yet simultaneous refusal to bend truth — both in His earthly ministry and ever since — offers a powerful blueprint that has always led people to repentance.

This is one of the most effective and persuasive evangelism tools, because, when you're kind to someone or when you go out of your way to serve them, it holds the power to change their beliefs about you and, in turn, the eternal.

Many times, we think the best approach is to immediately launch into what's wrong, evil, ill-placed, or diabolical about someone's life or path. While sin must be appropriately addressed, and there are times we must lead with it, and while we must never conceal the truth for the sake of feelings, how we approach and attempt to help must be deeply contemplated.

We've unfortunately come to believe the best approach is always immediately and without abandon *telling* someone rather than slowly *showing* them the proper path forward. Our toxic social media and immediate information obsession hasn't helped these human impulses.

Rather than relationship-building and making people feel as though they belong, we sometimes accidentally tear down bridges or build unnecessary walls.

Again, make no mistake: this concept of belonging doesn't mean ignoring sin. I can't emphasize that enough. It's not saying, "I accept your pornography, fornication, homosexuality, or adultery." It's simply making it unceasingly clear you will serve and help the individual regardless of their sin; it's sending the message you love and care, no matter what.

Love is a verb best lived out through demonstration, and, when properly exemplified, it never fails. In fact, it holds the power to change hearts, minds, beliefs, and eternal lives when the power of the Gospel is simultaneously delivered and driven home.

We're not called to shout or demean the sin out of people; we're called to lovingly — and truthfully — point people toward the Messiah. Colossians 4:5-6 makes this message clear, with the Apostle Paul writing the following about how believers should handle outsiders (KJV):

> Walk in wisdom toward them that are without, redeeming the time. Let your speech be always with grace, seasoned with salt, that ye may know how ye ought to answer every man.

Grace. Salt. Preparedness. These are the ingredients of a successful Christian's interactions, particularly when it comes to sharing the faith.

Evangelism is a covenant — a calling and promise kept no matter how an individual responds. There's no guarantee sharing one's faith will be easy, well-received, or even appreciated. History is replete with men and women who have lost their lives, homes, jobs, and families for daring to share the truth.

Yet we're still called to that covenant, regardless of the consequences. And, if we're honest, most of us in the West don't face anything too diabolical, finding ourselves most likely victim to eye rolls, mildly demeaning comments or being pushed outside of our comfort zones.

But regardless of the response and its level of intensity, we're called to share the Gospel and simply respond to any rebuttal with something along these lines: "I love you and you can't do anything about it! If you crucify me, I will simply pray the same prayer that Jesus did when He was dying on the cross: 'Father, forgive them; they don't know what they're doing.'"

This posture takes faith to build, but is essential to making people feel valued and embraced. True reliance on the Lord means following Jesus' example of allowing people to belong versus religion's attempts to force them to be clean before they can receive love.

FOLLOWING THE BLUEPRINT

We see Jesus throughout Scripture offer blueprints on how to strike this balance, but perhaps the best example is seen in John 8 when we encounter the woman caught in the act of adultery.

As the Bible explains, the woman was dragged into the temple courts early in the morning, with religious leaders attempting to shame and embarrass her while simultaneously working diligently to try and trap Jesus.

"The scribes and Pharisees brought unto [Jesus] a woman taken in adultery; and when they had set her in the midst, they say unto him, Master, this woman was taken in adultery, in the very act," verses 3-4 read, with verse 5 continuing (KJV), "Now Moses in the law commanded us, that such should be stoned: but what sayest thou?"

The religious leaders of the day, doing what they did best, sought to trip Christ up, with the Pharisees pondering whether He would disobey the Scriptures. GotQuestions.org offers a summary of the complexities surrounding what Jesus was faced with, considering Jewish law indeed called for stoning in cases of adultery:

> If Jesus recommended that the woman be released, He could be accused of breaking the law or of treating the Law of Moses nonchalantly. On the other hand, if Jesus recommended stoning the woman, He would be breaking Roman law, bringing on the wrath of the government and giving the Jewish leaders occasion to accuse Him.[48]

The irony, of course, was that Jesus proceeded to show them how to fulfill biblical truth, evading any such need to impede or violate the law in any relevant respect.

But before we delve into that part of the story, let's pause for a moment to discuss this woman, about whom we have very limited information. Most of us probably have questions: Was she a follower of Jesus? Did she have a firm relationship with the Lord? The primary

---

48 GotQuestions.org, "What Is the Story of the Woman Caught in Adultery?" GotQuestions.org, accessed February 9, 2025, https://www.gotquestions.org/woman-caught-in-adultery.html.

assumption is: likely not, especially considering what she had just been caught doing.

From what we know, she was a sinner caught in her transgressions and facing the consequences.

Now, let's review how Jesus responded to the woman and the religious leaders. He famously "stooped down" as John 8:6 (KJV) tells us, and started writing on the ground, acting as though He didn't hear the Pharisees' snare-trapping.

The religious leaders kept asking Christ their questions, though. And that's when Jesus delivered one of the most powerful verses on belonging and love: "He that is without sin among you, let him first cast a stone at her" (verse 7). It was a rhetorical check-mate, setting up a sure-fire loss for the Pharisees.

Christ then went back to writing on the ground. Many people have long speculated over what He was scribbling on the sand. Was He writing the Pharisees' secret sins out for all to see? Only those who were there know, but, whatever the message was, it shook them to the core.

Suddenly, the focus moved from the woman's sins to their own iniquity. The sound of rocks dropping to the ground in near-unison fashion must have been euphonic.

"And they which heard it, being convicted by their own conscience, went out one by one, beginning at the eldest, even unto the last," verse 9 reads. "And Jesus was left alone, and the woman standing in the midst."

It's a truly powerful image to picture these accusers rapidly scattering like pigs at the slaughter, the fog from the dust of their scampering, sandaled feet hovering in the air as Jesus and this woman stood alone in the haze, staring at one another, face-to-face.

Christ then rhetorically asked the woman where her accusers were.

"Woman, where are those thine accusers? Hath no man condemned thee?" he said, to which she replied, "No man, Lord." Then he delivered the most compassionate line of all: Neither do I condemn thee: go, and sin no more."

Imagine her thoughts as she stood in that moment next to Jesus — the Redeemer of all mankind — who loved her enough to allow her to belong to Him, blemishes and all. Christ invited her to belong to the God who would save her and love her.

When the woman looked around and suddenly saw no threat of death, did she believe, feel, and profoundly experience that Jesus loved her? One can't imagine thinking anything else, though we can't know for sure what happened next in her life.

But here's what we do know. The Lord is a bridegroom who came to save her — and all of humanity — from eternal death, and, on that day, He offered this adulterous woman His hand in marriage. While we can't be certain how her story ended, Jesus' interaction with her and His quest to allow her to belong offers a blueprint by which we can see how to do the same for others, helping their faith grow and blossom in the process.

As we round out this discussion, it's again necessary to highlight the last proclamation Jesus delivered to the woman: "Sin no more." Those three words didn't excuse, deny, endorse, or ignore her iniquities. In contrast, they condemned the sin and unequivocally called her to repentance — but not before she was able to *belong* to Him.

The spiritual "wedding" proposal Jesus gave her wasn't an invitation to be "married" to Him while still being adulterous and sinful; it was a call to transform her heart and fix her life on His standards.

Imagine a woman receives a marriage proposal from her fiancée and elatedly responds, "Sure, I'm happy to say 'I do' as long as I can keep my other lovers." Such a prospect would be pure insanity to any rational person.

Yet that's what's happening in some parts of the church today under the pretenses embraced by Woke Christianity, a patently false gospel impacting many believers. Too often "all are welcome" is translated to mean "stay as you are in perpetuity." But this isn't God's way; He offers His love and, in turn, calls us to die to self and learn to live for Him.

See, Jesus is doing many important things in the aforementioned story. He's showing He must be the highest authority in a believer's life. We can have no other gods before Christ. But He also demonstrates that His mercy allows us to *belong*.

This is the very reason Jesus said He desires mercy and not sacrifice. "But go ye and learn what that meaneth, I will have mercy, and not sacrifice," Jesus said in Matthew 9:13 (KJV). "For I am not come to call the righteous, but sinners to repentance."

Christ's grace is His free gift of power that changes us — if we embrace it.

All of it centers on starting the process with belonging. When we allow people to belong, we give them space and reason to believe, and, if the Holy Spirit takes root, thoughts, prayers, whims and, yes, behaviors are suddenly changed.

One of the biggest failures of modern-day evangelism is inverting or ignoring this pattern, aligning ourselves more with the Pharisees than we do with the love of Christ as demonstrated to the adulterous woman and many others like her.

THE POWER OF BELONGING

"Come, see a man who told me everything I ever did" (John 4:29, NIV). That was the exuberant message from a Samaritan woman whose encounter with Jesus at a well left her so spellbound she went into town and told everyone she could what she had seen and heard.

We know this is a woman who had an absolute train wreck of marriages, had spun a wheel of hopelessness, and was, at the time she encountered Christ, living in sin with a man who wasn't her husband.

Like the woman caught in adultery, this lady clearly had some skeletons in her closet — iniquities Jesus kindly confronted when He met her at a well in Sychar, a Samarian town. We see in the Gospel of John that Christ's interaction with the woman unfolded when He became tired and sat down to rest near Jacob's well.

Hardly a moment of mere happenstance, we can see the Lord was intentionally prepared to touch the heart of this Samaritan woman when He chose that location, setting her up for a life-altering interaction.

As the Bible recounts, Jesus asked her for a drink when she came to the location to draw water — and that request seemed to startle her. "How is it that thou, being a Jew, askest drink of me, which am a woman of Samaria?" she replied in John 4:9 (KJV).

It's perhaps essential to pause here for a moment, because the woman is raising an issue we must understand if we want to comprehend what's really unfolding in these Scriptures.

The Samaritans were essentially a mixture of Jew and Gentile, emerging during the time of the Assyrian captivity. After some Jews stayed back and married Assyrians, the Samaritans were the resulting people group of that intermingling.[49]

It's clear from Scripture that tensions eventually arose between the Samaritans and Jews, with differences in religious practices and other elements creating deep rifts.

These disparities were so intense, John 4:9 tells us that the Jews simply had "no dealings with the Samaritans."

"The Samaritans embraced a religion that was a mixture of Judaism and idolatry," GotQuestions.org notes. "Because the Israelite inhabitants of Samaria had intermarried with the foreigners and adopted their idolatrous religion, Samaritans were universally despised by the Jews."[50]

The history is complex and the context matters, especially to this interaction.

Jesus was most certainly aware of these dynamics, and yet He was openly asking this woman at the well for water. Her stunned reaction, of course, was rooted in the historical partings between her people and the Jews.

Christ, unconcerned with all of that baggage, simply saw the woman as a human being worthy of His love — nothing more, nothing less.

His decision to intentionally show up and interact with someone whom many Jews would disregard on the basis of ethnicity, alone, is notable. But once we learn more about the woman's story, we realize how her sinful life choices — and Jesus' reaction — can equip us in multiple areas.

The woman's shock over being asked for water is met with a powerful response from Jesus. He proclaims, "If thou knewest the gift of God, and who it is that saith to thee, Give me to drink; thou wouldest have asked of him, and he would have given thee living water" (John 4:10, KJV).

49 Don Stewart, "Why Is the Story of the Woman Caught in Adultery Missing from Many Ancient Manuscripts?" Blue Letter Bible, accessed February 9, 2025, https://www.blueletterbible.org/faq/don_stewart/don_stewart_1319.cfm.
50 GotQuestions.org, "Who Were the Samaritans?" GotQuestions.org, accessed February 9, 2025, https://www.gotquestions.org/Samaritans.html.

Here we see Christ in the process of once again exemplifying a belong, believe, and behave model of compassion. The woman, still clueless as to what He was truly saying, does start to ponder what this "living water" really means.

And, as the conversation unfolds, Christ makes it clear He's speaking about spiritual matters.

"Whosoever drinketh of this water shall thirst again. But whosoever drinketh of the water that I shall give him shall never thirst," Jesus said in verse 13 and 14, underscoring the power that comes from faith in Him. "But the water that I shall give him shall be in him a well of water springing up into everlasting life."

Jesus was obviously telling this woman He would give her a "drink" that would forever quench her thirst; He was offering to satisfy a desire within her that each and every human being has — to be loved, joyful, guilt-free, and forgiven.

There's truly nothing new under the sun, as these desires have always been embedded in the hearts of man, though many openly reject Jesus' love, a decision that can lead to profound unhappiness and, of course, eternal disconnect from the Lord.

The Bible tells us the wicked and those who choose to reject God will never really be joy-filled, as they roam about seeking truth and fulfillment in all the wrong places.

The longing in a lost person's soul for something deeper is the result of the so-called "God-shaped" hole begging to be filled through a relationship with Christ.

When we reject this gift, pain and confusion inevitably ensue.

In these circumstances — and in life more generally — compounded unhappiness tends to be driven by two main catalysts: hurt inflicted by others, and the hurt we have caused to those around us. These actions and reactions create a debt relationship we cannot pay.

All have sinned and fallen short of the one who has no debt, and that's the message Jesus is trying to deliver to the woman at the well. Mercy forgives our sins and grace pays all our debts forever, with true joy and peace taking root in our hearts and minds. It's a simple gift we must embrace if we want to experience these promises.

Now, let's unpack just a few more truths from this woman's

experience. Captivated and intrigued, she desired this water the Lord was offering.

As we reflect on these biblical chapters, it's essential we recognize that Jesus doesn't beat her down or demean her. Quite the contrary, by making her feel as though she belongs, He draws her in. It's then that He deals with her sin in the most compelling of ways.

In verse 16 — when she's ready in the midst of belonging to move into believing — Christ tells her to call her husband to come to them. Jesus, of course, was fully aware that this was an impossibility due to the woman's complex and colorful marital status.

"I have no husband," she said, to which Christ replied, "Thou hast well said, I have no husband: For thou hast had five husbands; and he whom thou now hast is not thy husband: in that saidst thou truly."

Jesus proved to her that He *knows* everything, delivering a word of knowledge surrounding her five divorces and the sin in which she was living. He knew she was angry, hurt, hopeless, and couldn't fix her circumstances on her own.

In those moments, one can imagine the shock and awe this woman experienced. There she is at the well trying to get water and this stranger has pinpointed with great precision the most complex, chaotic, and embarrassing area of her life.

We don't know what drove the woman's relational sins or what led to the dissolution of her marriages, but what we can be sure of is that marriage is a covenant before God — a coming together of one man and one woman for life.

This woman was seemingly attempting to live out that reality and yet repeatedly failed. While it's easy to judge the woman at the well for her inquities, the truth is: she's tragically relatable.

A Tragically Relatable Story

Many people today have gone the same route, becoming cavalier about marriage and relationships. Hollywood stars are infamous for quick marriages and rampant divorce, but the issue goes far beyond that, infecting almost every facet of culture.

Today, 78 percent of Americans believe divorce is morally

acceptable, up from 59 percent in 2001, and there's no indication those numbers are headed backward.[51]

Like anything else, a failure to understand God's design and His purposes can lead us in the wrong direction. The woman at the well very likely traumatically suffered a great deal of rejection just as many of us do; she also assuredly made plenty of poor decisions along the way.

Because Jesus knew this woman's sins, she immediately recognized He was, at the least, a prophet. But He quickly made it known He was the promised Messiah who had come to make every human being — not only this woman at the well — feel as though they *belonged.*

And that belonging immediately catapulted the woman into a totally different direction. I must emphasize here, too, that it was Christ's use of the miraculous in knowing the woman's sins that made a profound impact.

This brings us back to Christ's call for us to heal the sick, raise the dead, and use the power the Holy Spirit bestows upon us; these actions can help reel people into the faith. And that's exactly what unfolded in the case of the woman at the well.

We see her so impacted by the message that she leaves her water pot, heads into the city, and tells everyone she can about Jesus. In John 4:39-42 (KJV), we're told the woman's testimony sparked quite a bit of belief in others:

> And many of the Samaritans of that city believed on him for the saying of the woman, which testified, He told me all that ever I did. So when the Samaritans were come unto him, they besought him that he would tarry with them: and he abode there two days. And many more believed because of his own word;
>
> And said unto the woman: Now we believe, not because of thy saying: for we have heard him ourselves, and know that this is indeed the Christ, the Saviour of the world.

See, Jesus knew the woman's trauma from her rejection and her

---

51 Gallup, "Moral Issues," Gallup News, 2024, accessed February 9, 2025, https://news.gallup.com/poll/1681/moral-issues.aspx.

poor decision-making needed to be healed, so, for the first time, He allowed her to belong.

His interactions with her provide a great picture of how to be equipped for evangelism, with His use of the supernatural and kindness very likely leading her to repentance and replication, as she immediately headed out to tell everyone she had met about her encounter with the promised Messiah.

This story holds a key reminder for us all: Jesus lovingly gives mercy to the unrighteous and always confronts the self-righteous. The one who has been forgiven much, loves much. Self-righteous people don't love anyone but themselves.

Holy love is an unquenchable fire, but we risk putting out the flames if we don't approach people with love, kindness, and intent to help them belong.

It's, of course, easy to allow the fervor and excitement of evangelistically reaching people to cause us to falter in this area. After all, passion is fiery, but also a good thing.

Just consider this nifty parable of the two stoves: one stove is hot and the other one is cold. Which one would you use to cook with? The answer is obviously simple; you need the heat to appropriately cook any food — and the same idea applies to evangelism.

Can we really be a disciple of Christ if we have no fire to save the lost and are disinterested in their eternal whereabouts?

We would do well to understand this essential reality: There are people who believe in the Scriptures, tithe, and go to church every week and don't commit adultery. And yet some of these people lack the fire needed to ignite faith in others.

They are only "dating" and have not decided to be married to Jesus as the Scriptures require. The Lord proclaims, "If you love me, you will obey my commandments," and yet many decline these commands. The Pharisees and Jewish leaders would have fit well into this category.

And still others embrace God's call but forget to show love and grace. A balance is truly needed and, as indicated in this chapter, the best place to look for inspiration is Jesus Himself.

OUR FAILURE TO REMEMBER: SALVATION DOESN'T DEPEND ON US

~

Iℕ ᴀɴ ᴀɢᴇ of moral and spiritual confusion and an ever-quickening march toward the end of days, evangelism has become increasingly paramount. But when we're anxious and hyper-motivated to share the Gospel — all while feeling the intensifying pressures of cultural mayhem slowly boxing us in — it's easy to begin erring in our mindset and actions.

Some evangelists mistakenly come to believe peoples' salvation is wholly dependent upon *them* and not the Lord's grace and provision. Thus, the hustle and bustle of life mixed with the ever-ticking clock can lead some of us to take the burdens fully upon ourselves, turning the gift of evangelism into a cumbersome quest that becomes so intellectual it loses its heart.

And when our evangelizing under this paradigm doesn't go well or the results aren't what we wanted to see, disappointment can naturally ensue. As humans are prone to do, we make these efforts all about ourselves, failing to fully trust the Lord, and overlooking the clear and pertinent Scriptural guidance He has given to help us navigate the waters.

Before we continue, we've already established that Christ undoubtedly calls believers to spread the Gospel to all the world; that part of the equation is essential. We must be actively telling people about Jesus.

Building upon that clarion call, the key to evangelism — and the pattern and method through which it works — comes from a revelation delivered by the Apostle Paul. He told the Corinthian church that evangelism works in a systematic way: *plant, water, grow.*

What does that mean, exactly? Some people plant the message, others water and nourish it, but it's ultimately God who gives the fertilizer for spiritual metamorphosis.

It's this final step in the process that can often trip us up. One of the biggest mistakes we make in evangelism comes when we carry a misplaced belief that we can force the "growth" part of the equation.

Some of us might find ourselves getting into intellectual arguments with unbelievers in hopes of immediately converting them. Is it possible we might make compelling arguments that knock down spiritual walls? Absolutely. Might we be the final straw breaking the camel's back and shattering unbelief? Certainly.

But we're not going to argue and shout the Gospel message into someone's heart — at least not without God grabbing a hold of them and putting on His finishing touches.

When it comes to unlocking true heart change, the Holy Spirit is key. With a balance of truth and love, we're called to testify and share, predicating our message on Christ and delivering it with love, compassion, and unwavering goodness.

We must follow through on our call to share Jesus and then rest these efforts in the Holy Spirit's hands. Sadly, in the Western world, we have become very heavy on knowledge while going too light on listening to the Holy Spirit, particularly when it comes to sharing our faith.

In my 40 years of pastoring churches, I have seen a litany of evangelistic programs. Most are well-intentioned, but many lack a key tenet: teaching spiritual discernment regarding when to plant a seed, when to water that crop, and how to know when it's time for the Holy Spirit to bring a person to the harvest to be wedded to the Lord Jesus.

Many times, we're far too concerned with talking *at* people rather than listening to their needs and struggles. We assume we have to arrive with a theological treatise rather than meeting people where they are and journeying alongside them. So, what should we be doing? 1 Peter 3:15 (KJV) delivers some powerful truths that can guide us in this process:

> But sanctify the Lord God in your hearts: and be ready always to give an answer to every man that asketh you a reason of the hope that is in you with meekness and fear.

In addition to reminding us to "revere Christ," we're implored in this verse to "always be prepared to give an answer to everyone who asks you to give the reason for the hope that you have" (NIV).

This means always being ready to give an answer the Holy Spirit tells you to deliver. The more you desire to listen to the Holy Spirit, the more you will grow in learning to share the Gospel like Jesus did. This is also where the revelatory gifts of the Holy Spirit grow.

So, we must be equipped to offer intellectual and spiritual answers when warranted, but you'll want to specifically notice the Scripture gives us a few action steps to properly guide us in the plant, water, grow paradigm.

First, we're told to "be prepared" and ready; this means being in the Word and fully understanding the Hope in which we believe.

Second, we're told to be prepared *when people ask*. There are certainly times we must lead the charge and start the conversation by evangelizing and introducing the truth. It's important we're prepared to answer the spiritual hunger we'll be met with when we interact with unbelievers — a hunger that might come in the form of tough questions only knowledge with revelation can answer.

All of this, of course, is tied up with a bow in compassion and care for others.

See, it's the final piece of advice in 1 Peter 3:15 that brings us back to our need for love. The New International Version of the Bible tells us to do all of this in "gentleness and respect," with the King James Version using the words "meekness and fear."

Regardless of the precise language, the idea is the same; these words call us to a respectful tone that reflects the love of Christ. Rather than allowing intellectualism or frustration to cloud our evangelistic efforts — renegade elements that come when we make it about *our flesh* rather than the Lord's power — we must alter our approach and change our thinking.

The fear the Lord is the beginning of wisdom. That means we should be afraid of not saying what the Holy Spirit is conveying. We should be afraid of our flesh; our flesh loves to argue and get its own way and victory. Meekness is surrendering our mind to the voice of the Holy Spirit. The natural mind is sinful and hostile to the Holy Spirit and the mind of Christ.

1 Peter 3:16 progresses to drive home this notion, noting that speaking with meekness, fear, and kindness will give the believer "a good conscience." The Scripture continues, "Whereas they speak evil of you, as of evildoers, they may be ashamed that falsely accuse your good conversation in Christ" (KJV).

PLANT AND WATER

Often, one of the best ways to approach someone — and to engage in the "plant" and "water" portions of evangelism — is to ask an unbeliever who is in pain if you can pray for them.

We do not always know the season a person is in, nor can we discern the inner condition of one's heart. But we can always show up and offer to pray. Believe it or not, but most people appreciate it.

And when you pray for someone who does not believe in Jesus, you may be planting a seed or you may be watering a crop. Offering prayers for others is one of the most powerful and simple ways to impart and activate God's wisdom in their lives.

1 Thessalonians 5:16-17 (KJV) tells us to "pray without ceasing." And since we've called to seek the Lord in any and all circumstances — and we know He's always there willing to listen — we should be bold about kindly asking unbelievers if we can pray for them.

This not only helps open a door to God for these individuals, but it can also ease the stresses that can sometimes come with pursuing evangelistic opportunities.

Prayer can often be a more natural opportunity to talk to someone about Jesus, especially if we avoid the pitfalls that too often trip us up. In these moments, it's not uncommon to feel an immediate push to turn on a firehose of Scriptures as if we're equipping Christians who already believe in Jesus and know His Word.

Sometimes, the approach needs to be gentler and prayer is a simpler way in.

Make no mistake: I'm not saying you shouldn't share Bible verses if the door is open to do so, but you must have discernment from the Spirit, because many believers make the mistake of jumping the gun, kicking down the door, and trying to force their way in.

Not everyone is ready for that level of sharing.

When Jesus stands at the door and knocks, only the person on the receiving end can decide if they want to be grafted in. You can't force someone else's born-again experience; they must personally accept the invitation and invite Jesus in, and sometimes that process is slow.

Scripture plainly explains that the veil of confusion and chaos is lifted when one turns to the Lord (2 Corinthians 3:16-18). It's Him — not you — who opens eyes and hearts.

So, consider prayer as a powerful tool to help plant and water.

Beyond that, we sometimes plant seeds after feeling the Holy Spirit nudge us to simply tell someone, "Jesus loves you." This may seem trite and underdeveloped for many people, but do not underestimate the power of that seedling.

Knowing Scriptures and being able to cite them is important, but it's not always going to be your key to reaching the lost. In the end, it really depends on the circumstance and context.

Several times in my own life, I felt so barely nudged by the Holy Spirit that I could have easily doubted His gentle prompting to tell someone Jesus loves them. When I've obeyed that still, small voice, though, the person on the receiving end has often cried, become emotional, and said something along the lines of, "I told God today I needed a sign."

Some have told me they almost gave up on life and had been begging God for something to happen that would give them clarity and hope.

I've even had people say they were on the brink of suicide when these kind, simple words reminded them of their value to the Lord and snapped them out of their downward spiral. Words hold power and when we rely on God and not our own knowledge to form and utter them, we're sure to make the impact He's wanting.

These are just some of the priceless testimonies that show the power that comes when we obey the Holy Spirit and plant — or even water — seeds. There's nothing sweeping or major about these simple actions; prayer and Christ-focused promptings are kind and easy.

The truth is: we don't always know when we're planting or watering or how fruitful it will be, but what we do know is God promises to give the growth.

THE GROWTH DYNAMIC

I see the trajectory of the *pray, water, grow* dynamic in my own journey, as my mother began praying I would become a Christian well before I was born.

As a child, despite my father's atheism, my mother took me to a Methodist Church, building upon her prayer to plant and water. In fifth grade, I had a wonderful Presbyterian Sunday school teacher named Nancy Cheney who further nourished my spiritual roots.

Later, in junior high, my history teacher John Taylor told me about Jesus. And, in college, my football coach Mark Miller (a former quarterback for the Cleveland Browns and the Green Bay Packers) and campus pastor Bruce Montgomery went deeper into Christ's nature, with college peers helping infuse Gospel truth into my heart and mind.

These messages continued and were built upon in the pregame chapel services I attended, slowly opening my eyes to the reality of Christ.

Many years after my mother's initial prayers and the love so many poured into me, I gave my life to the Lord Jesus alone in my dormitory room and received the Holy Spirit.

Looking back, my question now is: who converted me? Which one of those many people — from teachers to coaches and Sunday school teachers — planted the Lord in my heart? Who watered — and who gave the growth?

The truth is: each person played a role and helped guide me along, but it was the Lord who inevitably opened the door and gently ushered me into salvation.

We must all be activated to pray, plant, and water, but we must allow the Holy Spirit to do the growing inside unbelievers' hearts. When we trust in Him to do the final work, we can release the burdens and pressures that might lead us to improperly rely too heavily on ourselves.

Our Failure to Rely on Prayer in Evangelism

⸺

W<small>E'VE ALREADY ESTABLISHED</small> the importance of prayer when planting and watering, but now we must address another related issue — our failure to rely on prayer as an evangelistic tool on the individual and corporate levels.

Before we dive in, a useful definition of prayer itself is warranted. Prayer is the sacrifice of our human power, will, and intellect to checkmating the devil by releasing the power of the Holy Spirit — it's placing reliance and trust in the Lord Jesus to move in people's hearts, minds, lives, and circumstances.

As I've witnessed throughout my decades in ministry, there's often an absence of prayer evangelism and a tendency toward preaching before praying.

Just as we might find ourselves preaching at someone incessantly instead of praying for them, we might also become complacent when it comes to regularly turning to the Lord for guidance on whom to reach, when to try, and how we're called to evangelize them.

When we forget to ask God to give us the grace or power to reach unbelievers, we're missing an essential evangelistic component. And in a lost and meandering culture, failing to seek God on these fronts is a surefire way to set ourselves up for failure, or, at the least, a lack of success in securing the spiritual tools needed to reach hearts.

As it is often said, "We have not because we asked not." We see this principle at play in James 4:1-3, which reads (KJV):

> From whence come wars and fightings among you? Come they not hence, even of your lusts that war in your members? Ye lust, and have not: ye kill, and desire to have, and cannot obtain: ye fight and war, yet ye have not, because ye ask not. Ye ask, and receive not, because ye ask amiss, that ye may consume it upon your lusts.

These Scriptures obviously deal with submission to the Lord. It's quite odd to think so many of us would go about the work of evangelism — trying to win people to Jesus — without prayerful surrender to God about the who, when, where, and why.

We see in these verses some important rhetorical questions about the impetus for fights, quarrels, and jealousy, with James proclaiming these proclivities and negative reactions come from the selfish desires within human hearts.

Not only does he warn against these ungodly sentiments, but he drives home that familiar mantra: "You don't have, because you have not asked God." And even when some ask, they find themselves failing to receive because they've inquired with the wrong motives.

These principles of surrendering to God, asking Him to do His will — and coming to Him with the right inclinations — apply to everything in life, including evangelism.

When we find ourselves fumbling and unsure of what to do in this space, it's often because we've allowed for an absence of prayer in our evangelism — a rift and space between us and the Lord that inevitably impacts our crop.

We know Jesus selectively called some real-life fishermen as disciples and the powerful connotations and parallel imagery rooted in that reality shouldn't be lost on us.

Christ Himself saw the connection between fishing for food and for hearts and explicitly noted it in Matthew 4 when He called Peter and Andrew into ministry.

"And Jesus, walking by the sea of Galilee, saw two brethren, Simon called Peter, and Andrew his brother, casting a net into the sea: for they were fishers," Matthew 4:18 (KJV) reads, with verses 19 and 20 continuing: "And he saith unto them, 'Follow me, and I will make you fishers of men.' And they straightway left their nets, and followed him."

I'm always partial to a good fishing metaphor, especially when it comes to evangelism, so indulge me for a moment as we explore how the practice can be applied to capturing hearts.

The first thing we must do to understand fishing is that it is not about luck. People who are good at catching fish are not randomly fortunate; they are astutely knowledgeable, using their experience and know-how to set up scenarios with the best possible chance of success.

When most unseasoned people go fishing, they likely pop a worm on a hook, throw it into the water, and stand by in hopes they get lucky and catch something.

Some people find themselves pretty disappointed when they fail to experience any tugs on the line and very few if any nibbles on their bait. Some will undoubtedly ponder why they're so spectacularly failing at nabbing fish, though the answer is quite simple.

One of the reasons many people don't catch fish is because they are casting their lines and nets in places where fish simply do not live or have no urge to reside.

Beyond misplaced locations, these failed fishermen tend to be fishing when the prey are not hungry. And the third simple reason some fail at fishing can be found in this painful reality: You can't make a fish eat food it doesn't like.

These same principles apply to evangelism and sharing the Gospel. We're often looking in the wrong places, we can sometimes use the wrong tactics, and sometimes we're prone to serving up a tone and message that misses the mark.

All of these errors are rooted in a failure to stay prayed up on the evangelistic front.

THE HEALING OF THE PURPLE THUMB

This reminds me of a miraculous story about prayer and healing — one that helps demonstrate God's power and our need to lean into seeking His will in our lives and ministries.

It was a cold, wintery day in Wauseon, Ohio, and I was tasked with getting groceries at the local yokel. As I was walking into Walmart — a familiar stomping ground for our family — I was greeted by a lady named Rita from my congregation.

We were well-acquainted as she had been in my small group Bible study for six years and her daughter Paige was in our youth group, but I wasn't aware at the time of a serious medical struggle she was facing.

As Rita was getting ready to check out with a full cart of groceries, she said, "Hello," donning her typical, jovial smile. But then her tone abruptly changed and she asked, "Have you heard what's going on with me?"

"No," I responded, unsure of what she was referencing. Then she held up her thumb and I was shocked to see it had turned completely purple.

It was so discolored it seemed as if it had a tourniquet cutting off the blood supply. But the thumb's appearance was the least of Rita's problems. She was facing serious medical complications that cut into her livelihood, as her finger issue was impeding her ability to write, placing her job in jeopardy.

As we talked, it became clear she was desperate and worried, as doctors didn't know what was causing the strange issue. I responded by asking if she wanted me to pray for her.

She looked to her left and then looked to her right, realizing I meant right then and there at the Walmart checkout counter — in front of God and everybody else perusing the aisles around us. No time like the present, right?

"Yes, I would," she said.

So, I got to right praying, commanding her thumb to be healed in Jesus' name. And you know what happened? *Absolutely nothing.* It was still purple even after our fervent prayer.

But I wasn't dissuaded. Rather than throwing in the towel, we prayed again just like Jesus did for a blind guy in Matthew 8.

See, here's the thing people sometimes forget or fail to understand about the power of prayer: Something always happens whenever we pray for healing, even if we don't see it. I believe that now more then ever, so, we commanded it to be healed in Jesus name a second time.

And you know what happened after the second prayer? *Again, absolutely nothing.* But we didn't give up.

One thing we sometimes see in Scripture when observing healing is God activating people's faith by asking them to do something they simply couldn't do before experiencing supernatural restoration.

A prime example is Jesus commanding the lame man to pick up his mat and walk — a total impossibility before his healing. In this case, I was about to ask Rita to use her thumb to grip on to my pen. So, I reached inside my coat to grab the writing utensil.

As I pulled out my pen and she reached for it, something incredible happened.

Instantly, in front of our very eyes, God completely healed that purple thumb and it miraculously — in that very moment — turned a completely normal hue. It was a stunning miracle that took place in the most surprising of places.

With all of us shedding joyful tears, Rita grabbed the pen and reached into her cart, snatched a box of Chex cereal and wrote on it, "I love you Jesus".

I said to Rita, "I will never look at a box of rice Chex the same way again!" See, the power of the Lord is available to us anywhere; we simply need to acknowledge it and eschew the lies that the gifts are no longer active or are only present in other geographic locations.

Miraculous, prayer-fuelled signs from the Lord aren't limited to Haiti, Zimbabwe, Malaysia, or any other foreign nation. That fateful day, the power of Jesus' name was fast at work inside of a rural Walmart in the heartland of America. Remember, the testimony of Jesus is the spirit of prophecy, as detailed in Revelation 19:10.

That verse reads (KJV): "And I fell at his feet to worship him. And he said unto me, See thou do it not: I am thy fellowservant, and of thy brethren that have the testimony of Jesus: worship God: for the testimony of Jesus is the spirit of prophecy."

Ultimately, we must truly understand the aforementioned simple truth: We do not have because we do not ask God. When we preach the Gospel without praying for God's guidance and for the lost to be saved, our preaching becomes offensive and ineffective. And when we refuse to seek God for healing, we equally miss out.

As James affirms, prayerlessness creates and breeds spiritual poverty. We've already addressed the powerful ways offering to pray for an unbeliever can open doors to the Gospel.

But our prayers on the evangelism front must also go deeper, with churches being the catalysts to equip, train, and lead the charge.

A Praying Church

When believers only pray for themselves and not the lost to be saved, what happens in our churches? The answer is right here in James 4: fights and quarrels.

Churches begin to die when the Christians who comprise them become self-centered consumers instead of Christ-driven disciples. The cynical nature, which negatively impacts individual and corporate evangelism, is characterized as follows:

- Prayerlessness for the lost
- Self-centered believers become consumers and demand getting their way
- Fights, quarrels, arguments, and church splits
- Competition between churches and church pride

While some of these issues create unique problems in church structures, those issues also tend to trickle down and inevitably impact Christians' ability to successfully evangelize. Prayerlessness, self-centeredness, and pride can eventually lead pastors and leaders to compromise the message of Christ to tickle ears and keep their people happy.

Under this paradigm, believers might start leading people to church instead of guiding them into a relationship with Jesus. When this happens, authentic evangelism falls to the wayside, as truth becomes eclipsed and concealed.

Without prayer and submitting to God, at best you end up with a facade that only slightly resembles authentic Christianity — and, at worst, you're left with Wokism, chaos, and an anti-gospel mantra parading as truth when it's nothing more than a tower of lies.

Mario Murillo, a well-known American evangelist whom I deeply respect, has lamented that a portion of the American church has become detached and distracted from its mission.

"Why did we get hung up on big screens, fog machines, and skinny jeans and think that God would bless that?" he once said, emphasizing the importance of relying on truth and not "tricks" or "impressing modern audiences."[52]

Murillo's right! Many churches and Christians find themselves slowly (or quickly, depending on the denomination) drifting away from biblical truth and into a cultural abyss. And one of the reasons is a collective loss of hearing the voice of the Holy Spirit in prayer.

Prayer for the lost is the process that aligns our hearts with God's will and launches the Holy Spirit to create a place where "fish" want to live. It can incubate a scenario that makes them hungry and leads them to take the bait so the Lord can "catch" them.

Evangelism or church existence without prayer is akin to making a cake without any flour. You put in most of the ingredients but without the key additive, none of it holds together; the same thing happens with prayer, evangelism, and healthy disciples. The demise of the American church is a primary example, as prayerlessness has bred spiritual poverty.

A simple rule is: if you don't pray for the lost, don't preach. After all, what's the point? But if you want the gift of evangelism, then ask God. Pray for it, because the reality is: He won't say "No." Don't listen to bad theology alleging the Lord doesn't want you to have that gift.

That's a lie from the pit to hell — a doctrine taught by demons. Believers who don't have the gift of evangelism lack it because they don't want it and haven't asked.

I understand being uncomfortable evangelizing or even being unsure of where to start. These are normal reactions for believers — especially for those new to the faith.

But that's why prayer for the lost and prayer for evangelistic gifts are

---

52 The History of the Bible: How Did We Get the Bible?, YouTube video, 1:21:21, May 9, 2020, accessed February 9, 2025, https://www.youtube.com/watch?v=cgAadaFQtjk.

so essential for individuals and churches who wish to live out Christ's example and fulfill the Great Commission.

If you've failed or erred in this area, it's time to reverse course. There is an old saying that goes like this: the size of the congregation for the Sunday morning service will show you how popular your church is. The size of your Sunday evening service will show you how popular your pastor is. The size of your prayer service will show you how popular your God is.

Churches today should be (and some fortunately already are) hosting prayer events and services, and encouraging congregants to pray for one another and for the lost.

I often wonder what might happen if a church suddenly announced, "We are going to get together and pray every week after Sunday morning service for the next six weeks. We are simply going to worship and pray for the lost." How would people react? What would the impact be?

Or, what if churches went out of their way to make an effort to set aside an evening each week and prayer for evangelism and the lost became a central focal point? The life change and heart transformation — both for the faithful and those who don't know the Lord — would be absolutely incredible.

It, again, all starts with submission to the Lord. 2 Chronicles 7:14 (KJV) reads:

> If my people, which are called by my name, shall humble themselves, and pray, and seek my face, and turn from their wicked ways; then will I hear from heaven, and will forgive their sin, and will heal their land.

Notice here God does not say that, if we pray, He will heal our land. To receive the requested healing, we have to pray with the right motives. We're called to humble ourselves, seek the Lord, and turn from our "wicked ways." It's all about the posture of our hearts.

And praying for the lost around us to find Jesus is obviously a "right" motive. How can we make disciples of all nations if we neglect prayer, or if the only reason we pray for the lost is to make our church bigger in size or stature?

We must seek the Lord and ask for His guidance as we navigate every part of the evangelistic process.

I'll close this chapter with an admission: I have been blessed over the last 40 years to have both attended and pastored many churches, and I can assure you of this: I have made plenty of mistakes when it comes to the role of prayer in my evangelistic outreaches.

Along the way, I've certainly come to learn the essentiality of prayer, but, if I'm honest, I spent a great deal of my ministry studying and teaching 95 percent of the time and praying only 5 percent of the time — and that troubling imbalance is far too prevalent in the church today.

The only way to catch a fish is to pray (equip and prepare) and then preach (act). The great evangelist Billy Graham was once essentially asked: "If he could only deliver one message to congregants, what would it be?" He quickly delivered a convicting response.[53]

"Tell the people to pray," Graham said. "Prayer is the most important thing we can ever do, and if I could do my ministry over again, I would pray more than I preached."[54]

What a powerful message for us all.

---

53 Life Action, "Five Things Billy Graham Did Not Do," Life Action, 2023, accessed February 9, 2025, https://lifeaction.org/five-things-billy-graham-did-not-do/.
54 Life Action, "Five Things Billy Graham Did Not Do."

Our Failure to Understand the Power of "Watering Holes" in Cities and Communities

ANOTHER AREA WHERE evangelism can sometimes go awry — or where there can be profound missed opportunities — surrounds coalescing and community gathering. A failure to understand the existence of "watering holes" can truly hamper the ability to spread the Gospel.

To begin, we must answer the obvious question: What is a watering hole? From a purely animalistic sense, it's very literally a hole from which animals drink water. But, in a human context, Merriam-Webster describes a watering hole as "a place where people gather socially."[55]

If you have ever watched animal behavior, you know you can always find them near a source of water. In Africa, there is a tremendous amount of film footage recorded of different animals living their lives in the wild. Much of this footage is naturally captured at the watering holes where beasts of all kinds come together.

---

55 Merriam-Webster, "Watering Hole," Merriam-Webster.com Dictionary, accessed February 9, 2025, https://www.merriam-webster.com/dictionary/watering%20hole.

Animals will always migrate from different locations to these watering holes, making it the ideal place to observe their interactions and presence. This reality is well-known and understood by photographers, researchers, and others seeking to observe.

And yet evangelists and Christians don't always realize how this concept translates to humans, specifically when it comes to the importance of pinpointing social waterholes in their communities and engaging people in compelling ways.

Once we've established the explanation and importance of waterholes, we must of course explore which locations are the prime social gathering places.

Without a doubt, one of the greatest watering holes in American communities are schools. Where else can you find such a high concentration of children with direct connection to their parents than in public school systems that often range from preschool through 12th grade?

There's a lot of debate today about public schools, and understandably so. As the quest to go Woke intensifies, curriculum and content sometimes become problematic. And parental rights are increasingly on the chopping block.

There's no doubt some of our public schools are serving up tainted "water," but the fact remains: our schools are one of the bedrock gathering places in our communities, serving millions of kids collectively across America.

To get an idea of the true size and scope, 49.4 million students were enrolled in public schools in 2021, with 1.4 million in pre-K, 32.6 million attending kindergarten through 8th grade, and 15.4 million attending high school.[56]

That's a boatload of kids — and we cannot forget their parents and guardians, the adults directly connected to them. See, watering holes like schools are essential to understand, because that's where the people naturally gather each and every day.

And if we want to find and reach the lost, we must go to these spaces rather than just expecting them to come to our churches.

---

56 National Center for Education Statistics, "Public School Enrollment," Condition of Education, May 2024, accessed February 9, 2025, https://nces. ed.gov/programs/coe/indicator/cga/public-school-enrollment.

Jesus, who spoke a great deal about serving others, said the "greatest among you will be a servant." One of the easiest ways to do a good deed — and to begin building the connective tissue that can lead to Gospel and evangelistic opportunities — is to serve at a watering hole.

How do you get in the door to create kingdom influence? Be a servant. Schools are always looking for volunteers to help in a variety of capacities. When it comes to evangelism, people sometimes look for massive arenas through which they can have influence.

While big platforms with the right motives and organizational affinity can be excellent vehicles for reaching the lost, the reality is that most evangelism is done one-on-one, with Christians sharing the Gospel message with an individual heart.

Taking time to serve the community at a watering hole like a public school is one way to open the door to such interactions. There are plenty of other watering holes as well, with the schools serving as just one example. But the point is: we need to think more granular and approach people where they naturally come together.

A LESSON FROM A LIZARD

Proverbs 30:24-28 (NIV) offers some insightful reminders about the power of one person to make a profound difference in the lives of others. These passages discuss four things that are "small" but are "extremely wise."[57]

"Ants are creatures of little strength, yet they store up their food in the summer," verse 25 reads, with verse 26 continuing: "Hyraxes are creatures of little power, yet they make their home in the crags."

The proceeding verses go on to note that locusts have "no king" but "advance together in ranks." Then, there's the lizards.

This chapter says a lizard is easily caught with the hand, but it is found in the king's palace. The revelation here is an easy one to comprehend. Let's first cover the broader idea captured in these verses: even the smallest among us can make the most sweeping impact for the Kingdom — and it all starts with showing up and engaging others.

---

57 Bible Gateway, "Proverbs 30, New International Version," Bible Gateway, accessed February 9, 2025, https://www.biblegateway.com/passage/?search=Proverbs+30&version=NIV.

Each of us serves an evangelistic purpose; no one is too small or too incapable of reaching others with the Gospel.

But there's another interesting lesson here worth noting, particularly when it comes to the king and the lizard. The king allows the lizard to live in the palace because it eats bugs; kings hate bugs in their palaces.

The lizard wants no money or power from the king; it is simply serving its purpose and, in the process, benefitting him.

Powerful armies cannot get into the king's palace because it is fortified and guarded to protect the king's authority and treasures, yet the small and meek lizard can reside there. Everyone has a selfish desire to possess what the king possesses: his position, his power, and his treasures. But the lizard shows up, does his job, and offers unassuming service to the king.

We can take a page from the lizard and intentionally show up at the watering holes in our community, authentically volunteering and offering our time while at the same time looking for powerful opportunities to share the hope of the Gospel – all for the sake of loving the lost.

The power of humility gets exalted in service. We see this in biblical proclamations such as those shared in Colossians 3:12 (KJV), which reads, "Put on therefore, as the elect of God, holy and beloved, bowels of mercies, kindness, humbleness of mind, meekness, longsuffering."

It's wonderful to run or participate in a ministry, but we often forget some of the best ministry happens in the most unlikely of places — and often at the watering holes.

Years ago, I served six seasons at a local high school as an assistant football coach. I took no payment from the school and simply offered my services. As a former college football player and a guy who's somewhat knowledgeable about the sport, I found a way to match my passion and experience to a felt need in the public school system (i.e. water hole).

It wasn't long before opportunities to spread the Gospel began to present themselves, with God using my willingness to serve as a football coach as an open door to reach young hearts and minds.

I distinctly remember a powerful moment during the first year of coaching when I was leading chapel services and one of our players came to Christ. He was a troubled kid who had daddy wounds and had already been in trouble with the law because of drugs.

But something happened that day that changed his eternal perspective. That young man openly gave his life to Christ, received the Holy Spirit and was publicly baptized.

That, alone, was a powerful scene — but it didn't end there.

He then, personally, by simply sharing his story, led 35 other boys from the football team to Christ and they, too, were baptized. It was the most beautiful game of human Dominos you could ever see, because God's goodness just multiplied from there.

Soon, other kids began to accept Christ and each story and encounter provided another opportunity to share and see the Lord grow His crop. Now, I pause here not to offer accolades or praise to myself, but to note something important.

At the time, life was busy for me; I could have said "no" to coaching or ignored God's prompting. But I decided to simply show up and serve, and how the Lord used that was incredible.

Schools, again, are just one of the many cultural watering holes we have today, with these physical locations offering us countless similar evangelistic opportunities. But another social gathering some of us might sometimes overlook — particularly when it comes to sharing our faith — is social media.

I understand not everyone is interested in spending time on Facebook, X, or any of the other countless platforms where people coalesce on these digital watering holes. But the reality is: hundreds of millions of people are on these sites and apps, many of them desperately seeking the Truth.

Others are simply looking for inspiration to live out their already cultivated faith. I can think of one powerful example of the latter scenario that unfolded during the desperation and uncertainty surrounding COVID-19.

At the time, the Holy Spirit led me to post a video on Facebook from the Psalms about God being a light in dark times — a pertinent message aimed at inspiring people to look to the Lord amid so much insanity.

As it turns out, Kathy Huner, mayor of the City of Wauseon where I live, is a wonderful Christian lady who holds the prestige of being the first Hispanic mayor of any city or town in Ohio. She felt a prompting during that time to turn on the city's Christmas star, a light display traditionally used to celebrate Christ's birth.

With COVID breaking out in March 2020 — months after Christmas — Huner felt God tell her that illuminating the star would be a powerful way to inspire beleaguered residents.

As it turns out, the mayor made this move after seeing my Facebook video about God being a light amid dark times at the exact same time God was speaking to her about putting the nostalgic Christmas star up to give people hope and encourage them to pray for our city and nation.

Not only did Huner end up illuminating the star, but she also launched an effort to encourage people to turn on their porch lights each day for a special time of corporate prayer for the city.

"[The mayor] is asking everyone to go outside (porch, backyard, etc.) and help 'light up' our community at 8:30 p.m. tonight and each night until the Stay-at-Home Order is lifted," a March 27, 2020, post on the city's Facebook page read. "This is to be done from home and not an event being held around the Star. During this unprecedented time this display of support and unity shows compassion for everyone affected by the COVID-19 crisis."[58]

That simple call launched three years of daily prayer for people and for our city, and also translated into powerful and inspiring actions, including the creation of murals, monies raised to beautify the community with flowers, and even an increase in the city's Christmas decorations.

The true spiritual scope, of course, went much deeper, as those daily prayers had power in the lives and hearts of everyone uttering them.

This all happened because Huner is a Christian servant to our city and God spoke to her about being a light in a time of darkness. All my

---

58 City of Wauseon, "LIGHT UP WAUSEON! Mayor Huner has requested that the Wauseon Star be put back up in South Park and lit. She is asking everyone to go outside...," Facebook, December 2018, accessed February 9, 2025, https://www.facebook.com/cityofwauseon/photos/a.226438851243263/625787804641697/.

wife Shelly and I did was pray, obey God, and show up to the digital watering hole with a simple video.

These testimonies offer a powerful reminder that some of the most impactful life change and transformation in our cities will happen outside of the pews. Our hearts change inside the church when we obey Jesus and share the Gospel outside the church. The reality is: most non-believers will be reached in other societal spheres.

Unfortunately, many churches have the mindset that our job is to solely build our church and serve Christians in it, forgetting the call we have to go out to all nations and places to spread the Gospel.

When we overlook or misunderstand the importance of watering holes, we also risk slipping into an abyss in which the church isolates and spends its time complaining about what cities, towns, and officials do wrong. If this complaining spirit takes over, Christians and churches can end up with a reputation for being self-serving complainers bent on embracing an us verses them mentality.

And you can guess just how much that makes non-believers love Christians.

If we're truly going to make new disciples in our cities and nations, then we're going to have to release an army of lizards so that Christians can influence by serving and, in turn, help to create a more Christian culture in our cities and nations.

But if we refuse to show up, nothing happens. One of the saddest commentaries I've ever heard came from a leader of a city's chamber of commerce. He said something along the lines of, "I love all the churches in our city, but we can't get them to volunteer or help us. They only care about what's in it for them."

It was a truly heartbreaking proclamation and an indictment for those refusing or failing to show up and serve.

CALL TO SERVICE

When we look to Scripture, we see countless examples of — and calls to — service. Most importantly, there's Jesus' sacrifice, but the idea of stepping up to love and help others trends throughout the New and Old Testaments.

I look at Joseph's plight after he was thrown into a pit by his brothers and then sold to the Egyptians. Rather than being overtaken by anger and rage, he became a servant — one who was pure-hearted regardless of what he faced.

Even when Potiphar's wife pursued him to have sex with her, he served Potiphar by saying, "No!" and protecting his master. Tragically, he was falsely lied about, accused, and was put in prison unjustly for four years, despite ignoring her advances and doing what was right.

Again, Joseph continued to serve others while trapped unfairly behind bars. Finding himself in one of the most unpleasant of cultural watering holes, he came along fellow inmates and helped by interpreting dreams.

Eventually, through Joseph's kindness and service to others, Pharaoh saw his ability to serve naturally and supernaturally and made him the prince of Egypt.

Joseph actually offers a masterclass in how Christians can disciple towns, cities, and nations — and that shouldn't be lost on us.

You might be wondering, "Where do I start. I have no ties to a king, Pharaoh, or leader?" As you can see from my coaching and social media examples, you can make an impact in simple and pointed ways.

Every single Christian is in the realm of influence, with each of us having ties to at least some of the important spheres — religion, family, education, business, government, media and arts and entertainment.

These are all watering holes where the animals gather. When we begin to serve like Jesus, Joseph, and so many others in Scripture, we change the culture from the top down.

Plainly stated: To transform a kingdom, we must serve the King.

Part of understanding the importance of watering holes is realizing how God will use us in any circumstance — if we let Him. God, of course, doesn't need our permission to use our lives for His purposes, but when we resist Him, we often end up meandering into the wrong places.

Just like Job, we find ourselves lost, adrift, and gobbled up by the chaos of life.

But that's all avoidable if we simply listen to the Lord's promptings — and serve.

If we want to get into earthly throne rooms, we sometimes must make like the lizard and be willing to help others and "eat bugs." If we want to see the Lord act through us, we must embrace a servant's heart and go where the people naturally gather.

It is through serving — and being present — that the doors open not only to evangelism, but also to building up our own Christian character. A servant's heart is a cleansed and sanctified heart. This is why David prayed in Psalm 51:10 (KJV), "Create in me a clean heart, O God; and renew a right spirit within me."

There is great power in evangelism when we do it His way instead of ours — and that all starts with asking the Lord to guide our hearts and paths as we show up to social watering holes to meet people's most natural needs.

In the process, we'll assuredly have countless opportunities to share the Truth.

OUR FAILURE TO BELIEVE IN MIRACLES, SIGNS, AND WONDERS

O F COURSE, EVANGELISTIC blunders don't end there. One of the biggest barriers in the American church is the rampant sin of unbelief. Jesus said everything not done in faith is sin (Romans 14:23), yet many in the church today are seeking to live out the truth without any faith.

It's an oxymoron that leaves the believer without the bones and structure from which to build a vibrant faith walk. Like a vehicle without tires, we lack what we need but somehow still try to make the untenable functional.

Yet faith is the sacrifice of the power of worldly substance. It's the turning to of supernatural things unseen to defeat the enemy, ushering in the King's Gambit — a victory predicated on moves of God rather than the aimless whims of man.

See, no matter how moral a human being tries to behave on our best days, we are still sinners in need of a Savior. Our obedience to the law is for our benefit, but it does not *bring* us faith. We must always remember faith is the substance of everything God created — "the substance of things hoped for, the evidence of things not seen" (Hebrews 11:1, KJV).

Yet the unseen realm, miracles, signs, and wonders that carry over into our lives as believers are too often on the chopping block, ignored or even denied by believers. This conundrum started long ago but persists in our materialist age.

Many years ago, I was at a youth conference with a great preacher. His assignment was to preach evangelistic messages every morning.

And he took us into a prayer room and he said felt the Holy Spirit leading him to share a testimony he and 38 American high school students saw with their own eyes while on a missions trip in South America.

He recounted how the group was with a pastor there when they came across a wounded man who had been attacked by gangsters with machetes.

The pastor and his team gathered up the man, who was badly injured, and took him back to the village for medical care where they bandaged him up. Two or three weeks later, the man's scars and scabs were visible when the removed the wrappings — but he was alive.

That's the first miracle; the second miracle is one I'll never forget. This man who survived the machete attack had accepted Christ during his healing and wanted to be baptized. The problem? The only baptismal was a patch of swampy, stagnant water.

They took him to the stagnant pool, and the pastor asked my friend to assist him in the water. Now, my friend was a bit horrified. The water was so nasty even he didn't want to get in and he thought, "We can't take this guy in there. His scabs and wounds are going to get infected."

But the pastor assured him he would be fine.

Moments later, when they baptized him in the name of the Father, Son, and Holy Spirit and he confessed Christ as his Lord, he came out of the stagnant water and to the amazement of 38 American young people and a host of others from the village, every scab and marking on his body was instantaneously healed. The new convert began screaming, "Jesus is God! Jesus is God! He is my Lord!"

This is the sort of stunning miracle one never forgets — an experience a person would want to scream from the mountaintops. But my friend was disgusted and discouraged when he briefed some other American Christians and they skeptically pondered whether it was true and even questioned whether it might have been done by demons.

So, when my friend felt compelled to now share this at the conference we were attending, he asked for prayer because he felt intimidated and uncertainty over how it might be received. Under conviction and battling shame, he asked us to pray for him to have the courage to share the testimony during next service.

The Lord indeed gave him the courage to share and hundreds of young people came to Christ as a result. See, you can't achieve a spiritual checkmate if you're not willing to strategically move the pieces — to trust, obey, and share.

Had he not shared, hundreds of young people might have left that day without experiencing Christ. The fear sparked by others' unbelief almost prevented my friend from obediently sharing the miraculous.

Tragically, my father was seated behind two pastors listening to the testimony and he heard them say to each other, "I don't believe that's true." Some facets of Christianity have been turned into religion and have become so naturally minded they are hostile to the Holy Spirit, paving the way for deconstruction and the Woke religion of the New Age.

HOW WE GOT HERE

So, how did we get to this precarious place where some believers refuse to entertain the full power and majesty of the Lord?

With the age of reason and scientific discovery came a new conflict in the church — something called "Intellectual Christianity," a dynamic in which we get so consumed with details and facts that, somewhere along the line, we miss out on true belief.

Even after pastoring churches for decades, I'm sad to admit I was at one point studying the Scriptures incessantly and teaching them while simultaneously not fully believing them or understanding their practical application.

This is the precise reason why Pharisees, Sadducees, Levites, and experts in the law could study the Scriptures with intensity and somehow still not believe in Jesus. Their love for knowledge was born out of pride in being called experts by people; they knew the details, but didn't know how to employ the substance of their words.

Thus, they allowed the practical to eclipse the spiritual, elevating their human knowledge above truth. This incentivized them to rule over the people instead of serving them like Christ does. Jesus saw these leaders for what they were and called them "blind guides."

"But he answered and said, 'Every plant, which my heavenly Father hath not planted, shall be rooted up,'" Matthew 15:13 (KJV) reads, with verse 14 continuing, "Let them alone: they be blind leaders of the blind. And if the blind lead the blind, both shall fall into the ditch."

The sting reverberating throughout that proclamation can plainly be felt even centuries later — and we should take it to heart and ponder it. Then, we should ask: Where are we falling prey to the same pitfalls?

As I said, I have been a blind guide as a Christian pastor many times throughout the years. It's not something I wanted for my ministry, but I now see how it inadvertently happens when we get tricked into interpreting the Scriptures with our own human abilities instead of receiving revelation from the Holy Spirit to teach us what God really means.

An easy example of this is in Matthew 16 when Jesus asked His disciples an important question: "Who do people believe I am?"

All the intellectual attempts to explain failed, as they noted some thought He was a prophet or, more specifically, John the Baptist, Jeremiah, or even Elijah.

Only Peter got it right. He said, "Thou art the Christ, the Son of the living God." (Matthew 16:16, KJV). Don't miss this next part, as it's essential. Jesus responded by telling Peter he was blessed and noting this information was not revealed by man, but by the Lord. Matthew 16:17-19 (KJV) captures Jesus' words:

And Jesus answered and said unto him, Blessed art thou, Simon Barjona: for flesh and blood hath not revealed it unto thee, but my Father which is in heaven. And I say also unto thee, that thou art Peter, and upon this rock I will build my church; and the gates of hell shall not prevail against it. And I will give unto thee the keys of the kingdom of heaven: and whatsoever thou shalt bind on earth shall be bound in heaven: and whatsoever thou shalt loose on earth shall be loosed in heaven.

In other words, Jesus was telling Peter that the Holy Spirit taught and instructed him with this revelation knowledge — and this is available to believers today as well, despite some churches becoming so intellectualized they no longer recognize how the Lord wants to speak.

This is also why Paul prays for us to receive a spirit of wisdom and revelation to better know Christ. In Ephesians 1:18, he asks that the "eyes of our understanding" be enlightened and that people would know the "hope of his calling."

This arc continues throughout the New Testament, with 1 John 2:20-28 revealing that true believers have an anointing or ability from the Holy One that can teach and instruct us.

"But the anointing which you have received of him abides in you, and you need not that any man teach you," 1 John 2:27 (KJV adapted) reads. "But as the same anointing teaches you of all things, and is truth, and is no lie, and even as it has taught you, you shall abide in him."

The reason John says this is because we are to be dependent on the Holy Spirit to teach us revelation and knowledge from the Scriptures.

Yet too many people today have, like the Jewish leaders of old, missed the boat on this calling, relying on the self and intellectualism rather than the Spirit.

SPLITS AND SPLINTERS

This misunderstanding is why we have so many denominational splits over doctrine. Too much of the discussion is guided by man-made intellectual reasoning and not revelation from the Holy Spirit.

This has given birth to a doctrine taught by demons called cessationism. It is a theology that believes all the gifts of the Holy Spirit ceased after the apostles — an idea I flatly reject. One of the biggest challenges to this ideology is the reality that there were other people in the Scriptures who worked miracles *but were not apostles.*

And, even more glaringly, miracles, signs, and wonders are still happening all over the world today in increasing measure, despite what naysayers claim.

I remember years ago having a conversation with a Christian lady from South Africa and she asked me if I could explain the doctrine of cessation. Her father was a medical doctor and her mother was an accomplished businesswoman.

Not only did she come from a highly educated family, but she, herself, was well-educated. Yet she also saw the spiritual for what it is and was perplexed by those who denied the signs and wonders.

I then laughed and said, "I can explain it, but it will likely still make no sense to you." After all, this woman had experienced the fullness of the Gospel and seemed perplexed by the idea that professing Christians would deny it.

So, I shared the very basis of cessation doctrine, explaining 1 Corinthians 13:8-10, verses that speak about prophecies ceasing and tongues being "stilled." "When perfection comes," these verses proclaim, "these things will cease."

As I shared these verses, her face wrinkled up like Saran wrap. She was appalled, proclaiming, "How can they believe that? That makes no sense at all!" She added, "Obviously, perfection hasn't come yet, and knowledge hasn't disappeared even though we have the Bible."

I laughed and gently reminded her I had warned she wouldn't understand before she asked me to delve into it. She also stated the obvious: there are people worldwide in God's kingdom who speak in tongues, and people who prophesy — and get words of knowledge.

"What do these cessationists think about all of those people in God's kingdom?" she asked, an aura of perplexed confusion and awe overtaking her face.

I laughed and said, "They think they're all deceived."

Naturally, she wasn't amused. Now, you know what they say: we laugh so we don't cry. And while I made light of it in the moment, we must remember: these are very real and serious spiritual matters — issues I've made it my ministry to address.

There's a danger when we become confused or misled in this area — and it's something I experienced in my own journey. Unbelief, at its core, can harden our hearts, just as Jesus warned the Pharisees.

And a hardened heart is often the beginning of broken pathways and misunderstandings.

Such a state is characterized by behaving self-righteous and acting self-confident in our own abilities instead of the Holy Spirit's power. This can create an opening to be partnered with doctrines taught by demons, which then breeds legalism, division, and a false gospel.

There's no telling what can unfold when we confuse the power of truth and the Holy Spirit to elevate self with emotion above all else.

We see the rotten fruits of such moves with hyper-intellectualism and other social movements. In fact, this is also how demons gave birth to Woke Christianity. It is simply a manifestation of man trying to make the Bible say what he wants it to say instead of what God intends.

But it doesn't only happen among progressives; traditionalists also fall on the same sword.

A FAILED EVANGELISM

One reason evangelism has failed in the Western world is that we started doing it our way instead of Jesus' way. Remember, God came in human form to show us the prototype of how we are to live, yet many of us ignore His examples.

Christ also proclaimed something quite fascinating in John 14:12 (KJV): "Verily, verily, I say unto you, He that believeth on me, the works that I do shall he do also; and greater works than these shall he do; because I go unto my Father."

It doesn't seem miracles, signs, and wonders will cease; in fact, it appears Jesus is calling us to trust and obey — and follow in every way.

Sadly, many are missing that mark, particularly on the evangelism front.

Imagine this: you have a giant lion trap with a hair trigger and you bait it with...a head of iceberg lettuce. Will you catch a lion? The answer is a big fat, "No!" But if you tie up a live, helpless lamb, you better believe the lion will see a delicious meal and bound toward the trap.

Now, you've caught the lion!

That's what Jesus did on the cross; that was the King's Gambit. He used the right bait to catch the lion. But, many in the church today have reduced the lamb's method of evangelism to lettuce for lions.

In evangelism, we are the bait. Our calling is to become like the Lamb of God. When we submit to the Holy Spirit in faith, the lions will be drawn to us, and we catch them. Sounds simple enough, right? Well, it is.

The Lamb heals the sick, raises the dead, casts out demons, preaches the kingdom, and simply rejoices our names are written in heaven. We must return to the King's Gospel of His Kingdom and allow it to truly transform our hearts and minds.

When people experience the power of His presence, they believe, repent, give their life in marriage to the King, and they receive the Holy Spirit, which is the same fullness of His deity that raised Him from the dead.

We can't intellectualize or talk our way into these realities. The Apostle Paul did not say the Kingdom of God is a matter of word, but of power (1 Corinthians 4:20). And yet too many rely on the former and totally ignore or diminish the latter.

Do you know what non-Christians hear when we, as Christians, lack faith in Jesus' name and His power? *Boundless and fruitless babel that explains and frames but lacks anything of transformative substance.*

SEEING THE POWER MANIFEST

See, the power of God's word and Jesus' name contain the Holy Spirit's sway to remove the veil that blinds the minds of unbelievers.

I once had a young man who was going through some problems ask if he could come talk with me. He *believed* Jesus was real, but he had never been born again. So, we met in my small barn in front of a toasty, calming wood-burning stove.

He began to talk to me about some issues he was having, and then told me how angry he was at his mother who had abandoned him when he was a child. It was easy to see he was experiencing bitterness, so I shared with him the word of God from Matthew 18 about unforgiveness being an entry point for demons.

I also explained how important it was for him to forgive his mother, sharing how Jesus died on the cross for our sins and how we deserved to go to hell but were saved because Christ loves us.

As I led him through a prayer to forgive his mother, the situation inside the room immediately changed from calm and relaxing to, well, remarkably chilly. And I'm not speaking about a draft coming through.

This young man suddenly transformed in the darkest of ways, as demons instantly manifested and began to control him. He went from being properly seated and attentive to totally erratic and disconnected.

The man started to scream and went front down onto the concrete floor, putting his face directly on dirt and sawdust. Meanwhile, this large, 6-foot-4-inch man — who very likely clocked in around 340 pounds — remained uncontrollable on the floor.

I immediately commanded the demons out in Jesus' name and they exited. The guy sat back up in his chair and he proceeded to tell me more about some of the sins in his life, including participation in a sex club with three self-proclaimed witches who he believed had cursed him; these women said God hated him, and the demonic realm clearly found an entry point due to these activities.

I prayed with him to renounce this lie and to ask God for forgiveness — and he manifested again. Suddenly, his face was back down in the dirt and I was again commanding the demons to come out in Jesus' name.

Finally, *God set him free.*

Bewildered, the man sat back up in his chair and looked at me.

"What in the world just happened?" he said.

"Jesus loves you and He just set you free," I replied.

He stared at me for a moment in bewilderment before breaking the silence to ask me what he needed to do to be baptized. I explained the Gospel, unpacked the concept of repentance, and told him what it would mean to fully hand over his life to Christ. And we baptized him that very week and there was not a dry eye in the house.

This is just one example of how the power of God and following the way Jesus did evangelism is so much more effective than trying to simply verbally share Scripture with people.

Yes, explanations are important and have their place, but there's an important reality we see in this man's experience: Sometimes, spiritual hindrances prevent people from having childlike faith in Christ, and an act of faith — especially a miraculous one — can shatter any such impediments. We saw the same thing with Diedra earlier in the book.

The purpose of the spiritual gifts – which obviously have not ceased – is to dismantle a non-Christian's unbelief and bring unbelievers to a place of Gospel acceptance. Thus, we are commanded to eagerly desire the greater gifts, which build up others.

Jesus taught His 12 disciples to do what He did. They, in turn, taught others to go and preach, heal the sick, raise the dead, cast out demons, and baptize.

It's still the same Gospel and it will never change, regardless of what any pastor or theologian claims. Demons are still active as is the power to restrain them, but Kingdom power stretches well beyond the battle between good and evil.

HEALING IN EVANGELISM

I remember once participating in a counseling session with a lady and her husband who were going through some marital troubles. She believed in Jesus, but wasn't a Christian yet — meaning she identified as a nominal believer but hadn't yet fully turned her life over to the Lord.

Her second husband with whom she was seeking help with was an atheist.

Her story was quite tragic. Her first marriage was to a physically abusive man who pushed her down the stairs of their apartment when he found out she was pregnant.

She lost the baby and went through a very traumatic divorce. Later, she faced additional challenges when she developed a rare disease that doctors couldn't fully treat. The illness left the woman unable to lift her left arm.

Needless to say, these issues and the perils of this woman's past plummeted her into an even deeper depression during her second marriage.

As she shared the harrowing details with me, I felt the joy of the Lord and gently smiled. Looking back, I'm sure she must've been a bit alarmed by my flowery response, thinking my smile didn't quite match the difficult details of her story.

But I had been in situations like this before and knew where the conversation was going. I decided, in the moment, to engage her atheist husband.

"So, you don't believe in Jesus?" I said, making more of a statement than posing a question.

I proceeded to ask if he has been able to help his wife with her depression, to which he said he had not and felt "helpless."

"Well, God's not helpless; let's see if He'll help your wife," I replied.

He understandably looked pretty bewildered as I proceeded to do the very thing that made me smile: call upon Christ for healing.

In uttering the simplest prayer, I commanded her arm to be healed in Jesus' name. The woman allowed me to utter my prayer and I promptly asked her to try and lift her arm — and something miraculous happened.

Immediately, she shot it straight up above her head like she had the answer to a question in class. And she began to cry, realizing she had experienced something real, profound and supernatural — a real-life, immediate healing.

This story will certainly sound strange or unbelievable to a secular mind. But it was a very real experience, and one that left me, at the time, in a fit of…laughter. I know you might expect a difference reaction.

Sure, I was elated and in wonder, but I know God loves her more than I do. I simply felt deeply in my soul in the preceding moments that He would come through.

But the situation left me with giggles over the hilarity of her husband's reaction.

I turned to her perplexed atheist husband and said, "Why don't you explain that?"

I wish you could've seen his face. Bewildered and a bit like a deer in the headlights, he admitted he had no natural explanation and hadn't seen his wife raise her hand in such a way in quite some time.

They both left a bit uplifted and stunned by what unfolded.

And that was the last time I saw the couple, but, as I soon learned, their spiritual journey took quite a turn after that impromptu healing. About two weeks later, I bumped into a friend of the woman's and asked her how the couple was doing.

"My friend is now deep in the Bible and praying a lot," she said, adding that the husband, though not yet attending church, was praying with her at home. The man who didn't even believe God existed was suddenly talking to Him on a regular basis.

What do you think made an atheist start praying? It's simple: the name of Jesus is still a sure-fire method for healing the sick and preaching the Good News of the Kingdom of Christ. And there are times when that name — and miracles, signs and wonders — drive people toward the prize.

Now, consider this: what if I insisted on simply trying to get this man to say the sinner's prayer? What if I declined to believe healing was possible and just tried to talk her and her husband into the Kingdom? There might have been a very different, less spiritual end to the story.

Tragically, too many refuse to entertain these miracles and, in turn, do damage by leaving people trapped in their unbelief with no evidence of the eternal.

I do not wish at all to sound like I'm bashing the body of Christ. I love the church, but, in my early ministry, I was a former cessatioist who dismissed these very miracles.

I am grateful for God's mercy and His grace to guide me deeper in faith — and understanding — in the name of Jesus and in the power of the Holy Spirit. I now see the full scope of His power and recognize how it can transform others' hearts, minds, and lives.

RAISING THE DEAD IN EVANGELISM

We frequently hear people say, "It's a great day to be alive." It's an appreciation for the gift of life, and it's understandable.

The opposite of life is death, and the latter, for most, can seem pretty unpalatable. That's why so many people spend a lot of time and money trying to stay young and ward off the inevitable. It's an interesting dynamic considering Jesus is the only one who's been able to conquer death; no matter how hard we try, none of us can outrun its inevitability.

Sometimes, though, some of us can briefly escape its grasp, gain a second chance, and very literally be revived from the dead.

Years ago, I received a request to pray for a man who was in his 50s and was playing basketball at a local gymnasium. He had a heart attack — and died.

Bystanders tried to give him mouth-to-mouth resuscitation, but lifesaving measures did not work. By the time paramedics arrived and transferred him to the closest hospital in a nearby major city, he had been dead too long.

He was on life support and it wasn't looking good.

To make matters more complex, his wife was on a mission trip in Kenya when the incident unfolded. Needless to say, we contacted her and told her she needed to immediately come home, a quest that took her 24 hours.

As she made her way back to America, we spoke with four of the hospital's best cardiologists and they delivered a heartbreaking prognosis: the man had been gone too long and simply wouldn't survive.

"If you believe in miracles, you could pray for a miracle," the head doctor said. "But, even if that happened, he would be brain-dead. We have given him every kind of drug we have and have been unsuccessful; his lungs are completely full of fluid."

The doctors delivered the typical "I'm so sorry" you hear in these unfathomable circumstances when all hope seems evaporated.

Yet these doctors had little thought that God could raise the dead. Those miracles they referenced? We believed that God could raise the dead, but would He? That prayer they hinted at? It was our only hope.

After the tragic news was delivered, we turned the waiting room into a chapel of sorts. Me and the Christians who had gathered began to cry and pray.

This ailing man's salvation was my central concern. I knew he was not a Christian who didn't believe Jesus was resurrected from the dead. He had told his wife this many times. Ironically, she was a devout Christian who had, over the years, repeatedly preached to her husband and dragged him to church.

He had simply refused to embrace the Gospel.

The chaplain on the floor that night was a very nice lady who asked if I wanted to go back and pray for the man by his bedside. I'm a guy who believes in the power of prayer, but I'll admitt I felt a bit more sheepish than bold that night. Despite my internal hesitation, I said, "Sure."

So, she took me and our worship pastor back to his room to pray.

The scene inside the hospital room was nothing short of anxiety-inducing, as the life support machine pumped air loudly and ferociously, with the medical machines artificially moving his chest up and down in an effort to force breath into his lungs.

It all looked quite intimidating. But, in the midst of that chaos and intensity, the Holy Spirit spoke to my heart, imploring me to whisper two Scriptures in his ear.

The first was Philippians 4:13: "I can do all things through Christ who strengthens me" (NKJV). The second was Romans 10:9 (ESV): "If you confess with your mouth that Jesus is Lord and believe in your heart that God raised him from the dead, you will be saved."

I knelt down and complied with the Lord's call to share these verses. Then, I prayed for a miracle and for God to spare this man's wife any excessive sorrow.

We went home that night exhausted and emotionally drained, but knowing we had prayerfully responded to the ways God had called us. In addition to the primary issue of this man's survival, his wife was our church secretary and we were grappling with how this would impact operations.

We totally believed God could do the miracles, but we didn't know if He *would*.

The next day, the man's wife arrived home and immediately rushed to the hospital to pray over her husband, who was still on life support. She, too, was a prayer warrior — and all of these pleas to the Lord seemed to collectively shift something.

Miraculously, something totally unexpected happened on the third day: the man, defying all claims of what doctors said was likely or even possible, came back to life.

To top that stunner, he had absolutely no brain damage and his heart was somehow functioning even better than it had before the incident, leaving doctors totally astounded.

Exactly two weeks later, he even played softball!

But even more powerful than his physical healing was the spiritual transformation that followed. After the man came back from the dead, his wife asked, "Do you believe that Jesus was also raised from the dead?"

And that man — a guy who had spent much of his time avoiding church and ignoring his wife's promptings — wasted no time in answering affirmatively.

"Of course I do," he said. "The Lord raised me from the dead, didn't He?"

Once again, miracles, signs, and wonders played a role in bringing someone from darkness to light and from death to life in every remembrance of the word.

I will never forget the church service where this man was baptized by his wife, openly confessing Jesus Christ as his Lord and Savior. The whole church was weeping and praising the Lord. Everyone knew it was God who still raises the dead!

People even joked and called the guy "Lazarus," naming him after the biblical figure Jesus famously raised from the dead.

I guess that was appropriate considering all that happened. But, all that aside, here's what I know beyond the shadow of a doubt: no matter what some theologians or Bible talkers say, the name of Jesus is the same today, yesterday and forever. Philippians 4:13 — a verse that carries the reality we can do all things through the Lord who strengthens us — remains as true as it ever was.

God still does the impossible! We simply need to show up and trust.

The impact of a healing like the one this man experienced can be profound and can bring people to faith.

We see this in Scripture after Lazarus was raised from the dead. In John 11:43, Jesus proclaims, "Lazarus, come forth!" Immediately, Lazarus, who had been dead, came forth — a truly unbelievable sight, and a moment that immediately impacted those watching.

"Then many of the Jews which came to Mary, and had seen the things which Jesus did, believed on him," John 11:45 (KJV) reads.

That miracle led many to believe in Jesus; the same dynamic exists today.

Evangelism is way easier when we do it the way Jesus did instead of making our own programs or sidestepping the power we can encounter and see through His name.

Signs, wonders, and miracles provide proof God is real, active in our world, and that He doesn't show favoritism. That's a truth that sets us free.

Our Failure to Realize There Are Many Different Baits in the Tackle Box

I F YOU COULDN'T tell from the chapter title, we're continuing with our "fishing" metaphor as we explore yet another evangelistic pitfall: our tendency in the church to use only one bait to reach many different kinds of fish.

We've already established the Lord has made us fishers of men, yet we sometimes send Christians out ill-equipped to deal with the many types of personalities and evangelistic needs. Why, you ask? Well, when some churches train believers to share their faith, they make the mistake of solely teaching the "presentation Gospel" with no additional meat on the bones.

In many of our churches, we teach congregants how to recount the "Romans Road" moment — the Apostle Paul's stunning transformation from a persecutor of Christians to one of the most impactful faith-shapers in church history. It includes these sentiments:

- we've all sinned and fallen short of the glory of God
- but this is how we know God loves us because while we were yet sinners Christ died for us,
- the wages of sin is death but the gift of God is eternal life

- confess with your mouth Jesus as Lord, believe in your heart God raised Him from the dead, and all who call on the name of the Lord will be saved!

This is known as the gospel presentation through the book of Romans. But there's not a one-size-fits-all approach to adequately and sweepingly serve as the singular tool to bring truth into people's lives. Sharing Paul's Romans Road Gospel is just one way to share your faith with unbelievers, not the end-all-be-all.

When I talk about there being different baits in the tackle box, I'm really hitting on the importance of meeting people where they are as we try and help them comprehend and inevitably embrace the Gospel. Our effectiveness intensifies when we realize people have different needs and that we must adapt and adopt our tools and tactics to meet those conditions.

Just as different types of infections require specific antibiotics to usher in true healing, so, too, do we need to vary up and diversify our "baits" in our proverbial evangelistic tackle box. We see Paul address this in 1 Corinthians 9:19-23 (KJV) when he discusses being a "servant" to all.

"For though I be free from all men, yet have I made myself servant unto all, that I might gain the more," he says in verse 19, continuing in verses 20-21: "And unto the Jews I became as a Jew, that I might gain the Jews; to them that are under the law, as under the law, that I might gain them that are under the law. To them that are without law, as without law, (being not without law to God, but under the law to Christ,) that I might gain them that are without law."

Paul continues by noting he became weak to the weak to "gain the weak" — and he doesn't stop there. He goes on to share the motivation for this adaptation.

"I am made all things to all men, that I might by all means save some," he continues. "And this I do for the Gospel's sake, that I might be partaker thereof with you" (verses 22-23).

As we read these Scriptures, we must ask ourselves: have we made ourselves "all things to all men" when it comes to evangelism? Are we on a truly introspective mission to save as many people as possible, appealing to each person's needs as we assess our approach and delivery of the Gospel?

As we seek to explore where we sometimes go wrong in this arena, I want to identify four different major types of evangelism so we can better understand our bait and better prepare each of our evangelistic tackle boxes.

Prayer evangelism is where evangelists begin. With this form of apostolic evangelism, we're combining prayer and evangelism to reach others with the message of the Gospel.

Next, we'll explore presence evangelism, which is simply the presence of God in your life in forming a relationship. It's displaying the kindness of God to others — a goodness that leads to repentance. When a believer first meets someone, he or she is called to be respectful and kind, taking time to ask the person about themselves.

The third type of evangelism we'll tackle is presentation evangelism, which is when the door is open for you to tell someone how to receive the Holy Spirit. The Bible tells us that if you confess with your mouth Jesus is Lord, and believe in your heart God raised him from the dead you will be saved, and that all who call on the name of the Lord will be saved. This "presentation" of the Gospel is essential.

Finally, power evangelism is the power of the Holy Spirit to be His witnesses. It is the empowerment of the Holy Spirit to heal the sick, raise the dead, cast out demons and destroy the works of the devil. The manifestations of the spirit draw people to Christ and His kingdom.

Apostolic Evangelism: Serving Like the Early Church

WHEN WE DISCUSS these various types of faith outreach, we sometimes use the term **apostolic evangelism.** The word "apostle" comes from the Greek word "apostolos," which means "person sent."

In the context of Jesus' early followers whom He sent out into all the world to spread the Gospel, this term is well known in the Scriptural context. But before its use in the New Testament, the term "apostolos" was used in regard to seafaring, with the word mostly referring to a transport vessel and the dispatching of fleets of ships.[59]

One can imagine ships going out into the water to transport items or even people — individuals with ideas, thoughts, and perspectives that could be spread upon arrival at intended destinations. The parallels to a person going out into the world to share biblical truth with the masses are quite easy to see.

More specifically, the word "apostolos" was reportedly used during the time of Demosthenes, a Greek orator who was born in 384 B.C.,

---

59 Ferdinand Hahn, "On the Origin of the Term 'Apostolos,'" Novum Testamentum 3, no. 1 (1959): 293–300, https://www.jstor.org/stable/43714117.

to refer to an admiral, his ship fleet, and crew, according to Renner Ministries.[60]

These vessels would look for places where civilization wasn't yet in existence and would land in various locations to "plant" new communities, taking their ideas and sentiments with them. This admiral would lead a troop[61] of people who were there to tackle all sorts of factors essential to the building of this new culture.

From road construction to education, each person served a purpose. In the end, these "apostles" brought their culture into new places, transforming the lives of natives who were already living there.

Just the same, Christian apostles took — and continue to take — on the role of changing hearts and minds with their tools, bringing people into accordance with the faith.

When you consider these parallels, you can see why Jesus used the term "apostle" to describe the work of His early followers to spread the Gospel. The Lord Jesus is the King now over all the Earth and has conquered Satan and his dark kingdom, with the Truth of the Gospel overtaking and pervading each person's life who chooses to accept it.

Heart-by-heart, God transforms human beings, with believers' evangelistic efforts laying the seeds of change. The Gospel of the Kingdom is apostolic in nature; efforts to share the truth spark a Jesus culture in individuals' hearts and the lifeblood of collective communities.

We see Peter speaking to a crowd on the Day of Pentecost, addressing the multitude and sharing the truth of what was unfolding before them. When Peter pleaded with them and shared the Gospel, the people responded. In fact, Acts 2:41 tells us many "gladly received his word" and were baptized, with around 3,000 coming to faith.

"And they continued steadfastly in the apostles' doctrine and fellowship, and in breaking of bread, and in prayers," Acts 2:42 (KJV) continued.

Two thousand years later, we're called to use various evangelistic tools to help usher the same change into hearts and minds.

---

60 Rick Renner, "The Historical Meaning of the Word 'Apostle'," Renner Ministries, October 25, 2024, accessed February 9, 2025, https://renner.org/article/the-historical-meaning-of-the-word-apostle/.
61 Renner, "Historical Meaning of the Word 'Apostle'."

This, of course, is just one biblical example. Let's explore some of the other times when Paul boldly shared the Gospel:

- Gov. Felix and Gov. Porcius: In Acts 24:1-27, we see Paul in the crosshairs of religious leaders. With a plot to kill him afoot, he finds himself before Gov. Felix and is accused of stirring up riots among Jews and attempting to "profane" the temple. In this instance, Paul ended up in a truly precarious place. He could have panicked or burst into a tirade; instead, he calmly defended himself before Gov. Felix.

   We are then told that Paul took his opportunity while in prison and captivity to share Jesus Christ with Gov. Felix. The two often conversed, leading us to believe Paul was using this moment — as he had so many others — to try and make a change in the governor's life. We do know Gov. Felix left Paul in prison to do a favor to the Jews and that he was succeeded by Porcius Festus.

   Much remains murky on the finer details, though we can discern one thing: Paul was on a mission. He started the process of making a disciple in Gov. Felix, recognizing the full power of what would happen if he was able to convert him. If the governor became a Christian, decisions would suddenly start to shape a Jesus culture. Such a mentality is the top of the mountain of national influence. If you can change the mind of the king or leader, you can change the mind of a nation.

   We see Paul here engaging apostolic evangelism for two years while in prison, showing the Lord can truly use us anywhere. And while we don't know the result, we see Paul's persistence for the Gospel — and it should compel us to do the same no matter our circumstances.

- Gov. Festus: In Acts 25, we see the Jews haven't given up; they're still laying out their case against Paul, telling Festus — Felix's replacement — why they're up in arms. Again, charges are brought against Paul before Festus, with Scripture telling us the claims against him couldn't be proven. Paul again provided a calm defense, "Neither against the law of the Jews, nor against the temple, nor against Caesar have I committed any offense" (Acts 25:8, ESV).[62]

We know that here, too, Paul shared his beliefs about Jesus with this newfound governor. In recounting to King Agrippa and Bernice the issues unfolding with Paul, Festus explained that Paul believed Jesus was very much alive. Recapping the Jews' spat with Paul, he said: "Rather they had certain points of dispute with him about their own religion and about a certain Jesus, who was dead, but whom Paul asserted to be alive" (Acts 25:19, ESV).[63]

Again, we see Paul sharing the Gospel in a truly harrowing circumstance. Paul not only offers up his appeal with Festus, but he seeks to proclaim the Gospel to Caesar, the highest ruler in Rome. Then Festus sends him to King Agrippa.

- King Agrippa and Bernice: Something about Festus' story clearly intrigued King Agrippa and Bernice, as the king said he wanted to hear from Paul himself, yet another opportunity for top-of-the-mountain evangelism. What comes next is much pomp and ceremony, with Agrippa and Bernice bringing Paul into what sounds like a pretty intense room filled with prominent people.

Festus announces he has heard the claims against Paul but that Paul doesn't, in his view, deserve death. Then, King Agrippa allows Paul to speak and he takes the moment to deliver quite a powerful evangelistic message, explaining how he originally lived his life as a Pharisee but now found himself on trial due to his "hope in the promise made by God to our fathers" (Acts 26:6, ESV).[64]

From there, Paul shared how he was once a persecutor of Christians who aimed his actions against anything related to

62 Bible Gateway. "Acts 25, English Standard Version." Bible Gateway. Accessed February 9, 2025. https://www.biblegateway.com/passage/?search=Acts+25%3A8&version=ESV.
63 Bible Gateway, "Acts 25, ESV."
64 Bible Gateway, "Acts 26, English Standard Version," Bible Gateway, accessed February 9, 2025, https://www.biblegateway.com/passage/?search=Acts+25%3A8&version=ESV.

Jesus. "I not only locked up many of the saints in prison after receiving authority from the chief priests, but when they were put to death I cast my vote against them," Paul said in Acts 26:10, continuing in verse 11 (ESV): "And I punished them often in all the synagogues and tried to make them blaspheme, and in raging fury against them I persecuted them even to foreign cities."

There, with a captive audience of so many prominent people, Paul shared his Damascus road conversion, revealing details of Jesus' appearance to him, and his decision to change his ways from serving as an enemy of Christ to one of His most prevalent and effectual followers. This is one of the great secrets of evangelism sharing your testimony or your story with an unbeliever. When you're in a conversation with an unbeliever share with them a miraculous story or your conversion story. This builds faith in them. Paul told King Agrippa how he had since spent his life spreading the Gospel. At one point, Festus claimed Paul was out of his mind, to which Paul pushed back by affirming he was speaking the truth.

Making no bones about his intent, when King Agrippa seemed surprised Paul would hope to persuade the leader to embrace Christ with such little time to do so, Paul delivered a powerful line: "Whether short or long, I would to God that not only you but also all who hear me this day might become such as I am — except for these chains" (Acts 26:29, ESV).[65]

See, Paul's "ship" in this case was imprisonment. He wasn't brought by will into his circumstance, yet he was still intent on spreading the truth to those brought before him on the journey.

- Publius the Chief Official of Malta: Interestingly, King Agrippa notes that Paul would have been set free at that point had he not appealed to Caesar. We see in Acts 27 that Paul is then sent with other prisoners to set sail for Rome. Some notable events unfold here, including a shipwreck that lands Paul and other prisoners on Malta.

---

65 Bible Gateway, "Acts 26, ESV."

Again, Paul finds himself on a ship he didn't choose (literally) and at a place he didn't intend to be. Here, too, he engages in evangelistic efforts that truly stun the people of Malta. After a should-be-deadly snake bite — one in which a venomous viper injected its long, poisonous fangs into Paul's hand — he miraculously survives. Paul then finds himself in the company of a chief of the land named Publius, who entertained him and the prisoners. In turn, Paul showed up to help — and heal — Publius' father, who was sick with dysentery.

We're told in Acts 28 that Paul visited the man, laid hands on him, and healed him. This act left the people of Malta fascinated and activated to also seek healing. Suddenly, people all over the Island who had diseases were flooding to Paul and getting healed. The people responded by honoring Paul and those with him, opening the door to even more evangelism through that healing power.

- <u>Preaching Under Roman Guard:</u> One of the most compelling facets of Paul's ministry is that he simply never stopped sharing the Gospel. In the final years of the apostle's life, he preached under Roman guard because of his testimonies to the nations. His ministry proves that persistence is key and that apostolic evangelism holds the power to change individuals, cultures — and the world.

Paul preached the Gospel every day for the rest of his life without hindrance. And his final message — delivered in act and not words — was to give his life for the Gospel when he was believed to be executed by Nero the Caesar of Rome. The exact details of Paul's death[66] aren't definitively known, but tradition states he was beheaded in Rome.

His example of ceaseless love for others through the sharing of the Gospel and the acting out of signs and wonders provides a roadmap for us all.

---

66 Encyclopedia Britannica. "How Did St. Paul the Apostle Die?" Encyclopedia Britannica, accessed February 9, 2025. https://www.britannica.com/question/How-did-St-Paul-the-Apostle-die.

DEBUNKING A PERVASIVE LIE

As we reflect on Paul's efforts in the aforementioned portions of Acts — and before we explore the various types of apostolic evangelism more intensely — we must briefly confront a lie that has become far too prevalent among Christians: the increasingly popular claim that believers should not be involved or engaged in politics.

Many will argue something along the lines of: "Jesus' Kingdom is not of this world. We shouldn't focus on politics and should instead stay in our Gospel lane." While it's true we must always put God's truth first before anything else — including political proclivities — this argument in and of itself lacks biblical merit.

If Christians are to be totally disengaged from politics, why was the Apostle Paul and every other apostle often preaching to the highest-level politicians of their day? Can you name one prophet in the Old Covenant who did not give messages to the kings, thus having an intentional impact in a highly political culture?

The reality is: these men of valor were almost always speaking into the lives and hearts of leaders — or at least attempting to.

And they weren't doing it for money or power; instead, their motive was aimed at setting seeds that would lead to the flourishment of faith in these leaders' hearts and, in turn, a changed culture.

Saying that a Christian should not be involved in politics is like saying a Christian shouldn't be involved in church. It's frankly nonsensical. Politics are very much a part of the human experience, and the Christian Gospel — more than anything else in the history of existence — holds the ability to sway the cultural tides.

This is why the Bible tells us to pray for our leaders. These men and women at the helm of our nation, states, cities, and towns have the ability and authority to change our laws. When we pray, "God, please give our leaders a heart to know You and to make decisions that honor You," we find ourselves engaging in — and igniting — apostolic evangelism.

Rather than follow ill-informed advice to retract from politics, we must pray and share the Gospel with those who have authority in government. We must pray for our presidents and governors and all who are in authority to come to the saving knowledge of our Lord Jesus Christ.

Imagine the enemy's minions having this very same debate. Just consider a few questions: Does Satan get involved in politics? Does he preach his message to kings, presidents, governors, and authorities? The answer is a resounding, "Yes."

From government to Hollywood, media, and universities, the enemy is very much active and prowling.

"Go into all the world" does not mean, "Go into limited parts of the world" or "avoid the politicians." After all, how can these men and women hear the truth without a preacher delivering it? How can policy change come if blindness among those making the rules persists?

When you change the mind of the king, you change the trajectory of his "nation."

Now, we'll explore the first type of faith outreach — one that dovetails perfectly with this conversation: **prayer evangelism**.

Understanding Prayer Evangelism

~

T HE EASIEST WAY to understand how to get started reaching people for Christ is to do what Jesus told us to do — to pray. When we look at Scripture, we see The Lord's Prayer is the model Jesus taught us to pray "on Earth as it is in heaven."

What does this mean, you ask? The simple translation is that we're called to pray that everything on Earth would be converted back to the way it was all intended in the Garden of Eden — that we'll have a life without fear, pain, doubt, worry, sickness, poverty, and death.

Jesus teaches The Lord's Prayer formula in Matthew 6:9-13 and Luke 11:2-4 explaining that His outline is essentially a blueprint for how to invoke the Father. GotQuestions.org offers a helpful primer:

> Here is how it breaks down. "Our Father in heaven" is teaching us whom to address our prayers to — the Father. "Hallowed be your name" is telling us to worship God, and to praise Him for who He is. The phrase "your kingdom come, your will be done on earth as it is in heaven" is a reminder to us that we are to pray for God's plan in our lives and the world, not our own plan. We are to pray for God's will to be done, not for our desires. We are encouraged to ask God for the things we need

in "give us today our daily bread." "Forgive us our debts, as we also have forgiven our debtors" reminds us to confess our sins to God and to turn from them, and also to forgive others as God has forgiven us. The conclusion of the Lord's Prayer, "And lead us not into temptation, but deliver us from the evil one" is a plea for help in achieving victory over sin and a request for protection from the attacks of the devil.[67]

The power of prayer cannot be overstated. When we began to ask God to bless and heal our cities and nations — for these places to look like heaven — we offer a prayer after God's own heart, because this is ultimately His will and purpose.

In 2 Chronicles 7:14 (KJV), we are given a promise: "If my people, which are called by my name, shall humble themselves, and pray, and seek my face, and turn from their wicked ways; then will I hear from heaven, and will forgive their sin, and will heal their land."

Notice that the promise is not just "I will heal their bodies or their personal finances." It's not merely focused on individuals' lives; it's a message about the collective. The promise is "I will heal their entire city and nation."

We already know God can heal hearts and minds; this message reminds us that the Lord is also willing to remedy entire cultures — and that should be a comfort in the midst of chaotic societal winds.

This is where the activation of prayer evangelism comes into the conversation. The activation of prayer evangelism is simple. We begin evangelizing by obeying what Jesus taught us to do. He commanded us to pray for "workers." In the Gospels, Jesus essentially said, "See that the harvest is ripe, so pray to God to raise up workers" (Matthew 9:37-38).

The promise we have on the table is that, when we pray for our cities with a Kingdom mindset, our God of heaven and Earth — the one and only true God — will create evangelists to reach those who do not believe in Jesus.

We see this laid out in the entirety of Matthew 9:37-38 (KJV),

---

67 GotQuestions.org, "What Is the Lord's Prayer and Should We Pray It?" GotQuestions.org, accessed February 9, 2025, https://www.gotquestions.org/Lords-prayer.html.

which reads: "Then saith he unto his disciples, The harvest truly is plenteous, but the laborers are few; Pray ye therefore the Lord of the harvest, that he will send forth laborers into his harvest."

So, when it comes to prayer evangelism, there are a few key necessities. First, we must recognize the importance of seeking God on behalf of our culture, our cities, our states, and our nation. Second, we must ask the Lord to send evangelists out to accomplish evangelistic goals.

The Bible makes it clear that true collective change is possible, with Scripture also calling us each to a radical and unadulterated faith.

Christ uses a mustard seed to make a profound point about what's possible when we believe.

"[Jesus] said to them, "For truly, I say to you, if you have faith like a grain of mustard seed, you will say to this mountain, 'Move from here to there,' and it will move, and nothing will be impossible for you,'" Matthew 17:20 (ESV) reads.

And in Mark 4:30-32 (KJV), we see Jesus likening the Kingdom of God to a grain of mustard seed. Christ said it is "less than all the seeds that be in the earth: But when it is sown, it groweth up, and becometh greater than all herbs, and shooteth out great branches; so that the fowls of the air may lodge under the shadow of it."

These comparisons of spiritual matters and a mustard continue in Luke 13:18–19 and Luke 17:5-6 (KJV), with the latter reading, "And the apostles said unto the Lord, Increase our faith. And the Lord said, If you had faith as a grain of mustard seed, you might say unto this sycamore tree, be plucked up by the root, and be planted in the sea; and it should obey you."

What's most notable in these verses is that the small, round mustard seed is used by Christ to deliver a great promise — one that has mystified many throughout the ages.

It's an assurance that, if you have faith even as tiny as this seed, anything under the Lord is possible. That in mind, the promise embedded in these verses is simple — and essential — when it comes to prayer evangelism.

If you can activate the smallest, the most miniscule and microscopic prayer, and faithfully ask it, God can do immeasurably more than we could ever ask or imagine. We often fail to remember this in or our own lives and certainly don't apply it enough when it comes to delivering prayers for our cities, towns, and broader communities.

The easiest activation for prayer evangelism is to speak to the Lord, saying something along the lines of: "God help my city believe in Jesus." It's a simple prayer that can yield massive results — and its one we see executed in Scripture.

POWERFUL EXAMPLES OF PRAYER EVANGELISM

A testimony closest to my heart would be the conversion of my father who was an atheist drug cop. He battled his own demons because of severe abuse from his father and witnessing, working around — and suffering — the toughest facets of society's evils.

Because of this, he would allow no one even to speak with him about Jesus. To offer an example showing the extent of the problem, a friend of mine who had just become a Christian tried to share his testimony with my father and he threatened to kick him out of our house if he spoke anymore about Christ.

Knowing this barrier, we prayed and gathered people to pray for him as well. After three years of praying for his soul, a miracle happened. While driving his police cruiser the Holy Spirit came upon him so strongly he had to pull over on the side of the street where he began weeping uncontrollably.

That evening at 7 p.m., he went into a meeting to do a drug speech — something that was part of his job. But this time — after that encounter with the Lord — something was very different. He said, "When I looked at those people, I never felt a love like that ever." He added, "I knew it was the Lord."

My dad was remarkably converted in one encounter with no one talking to him in his police cruiser or before the drug speech. It was all the Lord. He was baptized the next week, affirming these beliefs and experiences.

And, throughout his life, he lived out these Christian values. Before my father died and went to heaven, he preached 18 years at a nursing home, ran a food ministry, and passed out Bibles in Red Square, Moscow to KGB policeman.

When we pray for souls, God answers those calls!

A great picture of a faithful servant of God is Daniel, an Old Testament prayer evangelist who clung to the Lord no matter the cost. Daniel prayed three times a day facing Jerusalem — and that's not all. He asked God that the Jewish people would become believers, stop worshipping Pagan gods, and for the Lord to heal their land.

Considering the Jewish people were experiencing the Babylonian captivity at the time — a period from 607 to 586 B.C. when King Nebuchadnezzar II of Babylon took them away from their land and essentially held them hostage — Daniel's prayers were understandably fervent.[68]

As a faithful man, he knew his invocations and devotion were desperately needed. Israel was being judged by God for idolatry and for turning against the Lord, and the dangers were paramount.

Nebuchadnezzar's incursions led to the destruction of the Jewish temple and Jerusalem; many were killed and others' lives were totally upended along the way.[69] Daniel, though, remained spiritually resolute, desperately attempting to call his people back to the Lord.

One of the great pictures we have of spiritual warfare in the heavenly realms is in the Book of Daniel, chapters nine and 10, as we see the potential power of prayer in action. This portion of Scripture offers a picture God gives us of Daniel's prayer being immediately launched to God as soon as it was uttered.

"I set my face unto the Lord God, to seek by prayer and supplications, with fasting, and sackcloth, and ashes," Daniel 9:3 (KJV) reads, with verse 4 continuing, "And I prayed unto the Lord my God, and made my confession, and said, O Lord, the great and dreadful God, keeping the covenant and mercy to them that love him, and to them that keep his commandments."

We see here that Daniel didn't give up; when his people failed to live up to their calling to the Lord, he turned to prayer to seek God's forgiveness, admit collective fault, and to try to spiritually right a ship that was moving full-speed in the wrong direction.

---

68 GotQuestions.org, "What Was the Babylonian Captivity/Exile?" GotQuestions.org, accessed February 9, 2025, https://www.gotquestions.org/Babylonian-captivity-exile.html.
69 GotQuestions.org, "Babylonian Captivity/Exile."

Notice Daniel also didn't hedge, ignore the Israelis' errors, or look for excuses; he confronted his people's responsibility head-on.

"We have sinned, and have committed iniquity, and have done wickedly, and have rebelled, even by departing from thy precepts and from thy judgments," he said in verse 5 (KJV), continuing by acknowledging how God had driven his people out of their land due to their trespasses.

Daniel believed in the power of prayer, as he said in Daniel 9:13 that the evils his people had brought upon themselves could be turned from by understanding the Lord's truth. In the midst of the self-imposed pain and suffering, Daniel admitted, "for we obeyed not [God's] voice" (verse 14) and that they had "sinned...[and] done wickedly" (verse 15).

In acknowledging these realities, Daniel implored God to forgive Israel and to hear his desperate prayers on behalf of his people.

"O Lord, according to all thy righteousness, I beseech thee, let thine anger and thy fury be turned away from thy city Jerusalem, thy holy mountain: because for our sins, and for the iniquities of our fathers, Jerusalem and thy people are become a reproach to all that are about us," Daniel said in verse 16, asking the Lord to "hear the prayer of thy servant" and to "forgive" in the subsequent Scriptures.

As he was offering these intense prayers, Daniel then recounted how Gabriel came to him to share how Daniel's prayer sparked "a word" that went out as soon as Daniel's invocation began.

Gabriel then gave a prophetic vision to Daniel, as we see in chapter 9 — a Messianic and eschatological prophecy that is incredibly detailed and has sparked various theories and ideas posited by theologians.

Regardless of those opinions and interpretations, we see something quite clear and undisputed: Daniel's prayer was so powerful it sparked one of the most detailed prophecies in all of the Old Testament.

Entire anthologies can be written on Daniel and the prophecies unveiled following these prayers, but let's ponder, for a moment, the blueprint which he set into motion – a call for all of us to seek the Lord diligently on behalf or our towns, cities, communities and even our nation.

Praying in Tongues (A.K.A.: Praying in the Spirit)

One of the most controversial — yet desperately needed – elements of prayer evangelism is praying in tongues.

Despite the debate that often rages in the church today, the Apostle Paul clearly indicates God's will for us to pray in tongues.

Acts shows how the early church started praying in tongues at Pentecost — and the practice simply grew from there, extending throughout the last two millennia and continuing today. Praying in tongues is vital, essential, and intended for all believers.

Here are some of the benefits:

- When we speak in tongues, the devil does not understand our prayer line. Thus, he cannot attack it.
- When we pray in tongues, it is an act of total devotion; it's 100% faith, which is the circumcision and removal of flesh from the brain.
- It's impossible to pray without ceasing if we don't pray in the Spirit. We run out of things to pray for easily, and tongues offers a spiritual pathway to connect with the Lord that extends our typical prayer life.

The rejection of praying in tongues can lead to some dire spiritual circumstances, including to a material Christianity devoid of the supernatural, to dead works, and to wrong judgments about other believers.

Taken to the extreme, these sentiments can lead to division, deconstruction, Woke Christianity, and shipwrecked faith. We must hold fast that praying in tongues is not only biblical — but also God's will for believers.

It has been my experience, more than anything, that praying in tongues is the key to supernatural evangelism.

Some of the greatest evangelists that we can think of all share one common prayer denominator: they prayed in tongues as the Bible indicated. When we sacrifice the power of our brain and reject obsessive materialism, praying in tongues becomes a King's Gambit and a powerful, game-ending checkmate to the devil.

If you're not sure where to start — or if you've been closed off to it, consider turning to God and seeking Him to add another weapon to destroy the works of the devil.

Always remember Jesus is our theology. How many gifts did Jesus have? When you accept Christ into your heart where does He live? In you! Therefore; how many gifts do you have? All of them! Just ask God for the faith to pray in tongues — and He will answer!

Now, let's get back to Daniel and his prayerful examples.

AMERICA MIRRORING ISRAEL

America, in many ways, mirrors the lostness and waywardness of Daniel's people, as many today have lost their way. Culture is embracing a collective ideology predicated on the self rather than God's eternal truth, with morals and values falling to the wayside.

From Wokism to loosened sexual views and practices, Judeo-Christian ethics have continued to evaporate as people buy into the lie that they're the arbiters of their own truths. It's easy amid the mixture of chaotic sights and sounds to wring our hands and complain – to rant and rave as our TV screens expose the depths of our moral depravity.

But Daniel provides another path forward: a prayerful response. He recognized the horrific state of his culture and, rather than ignore it, scream and yell, or offer some other toxic and unhelpful reaction, he turned to God in prayer, seeking changed hearts and minds.

That's exactly what prayer evangelism calls us to, with Daniel serving as a prime example of how we can seek the Lord and truth by invoking His name and admitting our sins.

We see such dynamics play out in other parts of Scripture as well. In Luke 2, when Mary and Joseph take Jesus to Jerusalem to present Him to God, they encounter a man named Simeon, whom Scripture describes as "righteous and devout."

See, Simeon had waited for quite some time for the Lord, very likely praying for the Messiah's coming after being told by God it would happen during his lifetime. "It had been revealed to him by the Holy Spirit that he would not die before he had seen the Lord's Messiah," Luke 2:26 (KJV) reads, with verse 27 continuing, "Moved by the Spirit, he went into the temple courts. When the parents brought in the child Jesus to do for him what the custom of the Law required, Simeon took him in his arms and praised God."

It's powerful to see how Simeon's earnest prayer for what God had promised turned from expectancy to gratitude, as he honored the Lord when the transformational promise of Jesus' arrival came to fruition.

Verses 29-32 capture what Simeon told God in response to its fulfillment:

> "Sovereign Lord, as you have promised, you may now dismiss[d] your servant in peace. For my eyes have seen your salvation, which you have prepared in the sight of all nations: a light for revelation to the Gentiles, and the glory of your people Israel."

In that same chapter, we're introduced to Anna, a prophet who is described as quite elderly and devout. This 84-year-old widow delivers a timeless masterclass in the art of prayer evangelism, with the Bible telling us she worshipped and prayed night and day in the temple.

"She never left the temple but worshiped night and day, fasting and praying," Luke 2:37 (KJV) reads.

And Anna's prayers were answered when Jesus was brought to her in the very place she had been incessantly seeking the Lord. She immediately reacted after realizing, like Simeon, God's promised child had arrived.

"And she coming in that instant gave thanks likewise unto the Lord, and spake of him to all them that looked for redemption in Jerusalem," verse 38 reads.

This is a great example of how Jesus can be born into the lives of people. Anna was a Kingdom prayer evangelist and her devotion shows the type of prayer warriors each of us are called to be.

Stories surrounding powerful prayer evangelists like Daniel, Simeon, and Anna are spread throughout the biblical narrative, with various personalities — and circumstances — showing the many different ways this type of evangelism takes form.

Another one of the most powerful pictures of prayer evangelism is in Acts 4 after we see Peter and John before the Sanhedrin. These religious leaders were "disturbed" after the men started speaking to the people about Jesus and the "resurrection of the dead."

In fact, they were so perturbed they put Peter and John in jail, but it didn't matter because many of those who heard the Gospel from them believed it, with the total number of men embracing the Truth swelling to 5,000.

Peter and John, of course, faced questions and scrutiny from the religious leaders who demanded to know why they were preaching and by what authority they shared with the people. At the center of some of the discontent seemed to be the healing of a man who was "lame."

The miracle teamed with Peter and John powerfully sharing the Gospel left the religious leaders shocked and unsure of what to do. The leaders told the men to stop proclaiming the Truth, but Peter and John hit back in Acts 4:19-20 (NIV)[70], essentially saying: "What's right in the Lord's eyes — for us to listen to you or to God? You be the judges of that! As for the two of us, we can't stop speaking about the powerful truth we've heard and seen!"

The religious leaders, of course, continued their threats but ended up letting Peter and John go. After all, the people were believing them and the man's miracle healing offered physical evidence that Jesus' followers were on to something real and authentic.

Peter and John, surely enthusiastic about what had unfolded after their boldness — went back to their fellow believers, and when the Christian cohort gathered together to pray, God not only answered their prayer, but the place where they were standing literally shook.

Acts 4:31 (KJV) reads, "And when they had prayed, the place was shaken where they were assembled together; and they were all filled with the Holy Ghost, and they spake the word of God with boldness."

You might call it a sign and a wonder that such an earthquake unfolded as the result of prayer. In some ways, it is quite humorous to think fervent prayer might have left the local building and grounds committee with some cracks and patchwork to fix.

In the end, their prayer was a Kingdom evangelist prayer quoting a promise from Psalms — "Why do the nations rage." These early believers were praying a warfare prayer in the heavenly realms that shook the nations.

---

70 Bible Gateway, "Acts 4:19–20, New International Version," Bible Gateway, accessed February 9, 2025, https://www.biblegateway.com/passage/?search=Acts+4%3A19-20&version=NIV.

Just ponder the context: They were experiencing extreme persecution because Jesus came, died, and resurrected, becoming King over Lucifer and the dark kingdom. The believers prayed and more and more people believed in Jesus as the savior of the world.

There's a powerful lesson here for us, too, as we navigate an ailing culture that heralds and props up untruth, Wokism, and diabolical lies. We can — and should — offer similar prayers for the people and culture around us.

Jesus and Prayer Evangelism

An incredibly simple activation of prayer evangelism can come by asking God something basic like, "Lord, please help people believe in Jesus." We see Christ Himself exemplify prayer evangelism in John 17, offering a model of this form of furthering the Gospel for us to emulate.

In this chapter, He simply prayed that people would believe in Him while also praying for the future messages that would later be preached in His name. He prays about Himself, for the disciples, and then believers more generally.

At the start of the chapter, Christ proclaims, "Father, the hour is come; glorify thy Son, that thy Son also may glorify thee" (KJV).

"As thou hast given him power over all flesh, that he should give eternal life to as many as thou hast given him," verse 2 continues, with verse 3 adding, "And this is life eternal, that they might know thee the only true God, and Jesus Christ, whom thou hast sent."

Jesus progresses from there to pray for His disciples, asking the Lord to protect them and "keep them from … evil" (verse 15)

"They are not of the world, even as I am not of the world," Jesus continued. "Sanctify them through thy truth: thy word is truth."

As Christ rounds out His prayer, He transitions from the disciples to those who come to believe in Him through the disciples' sharing and that those who hear the truth will see and believe the powerful Gospel message.

"That they all may be one; as thou, Father, art in me, and I in thee, that they also may be one in us," Jesus said in verse 21. "That the world may believe that thou hast sent me."

Christ's prayer evangelism is on full display as He seeks the whole world's knowledge of His coming and God's love. We, too, can — and must — engage in the same types of prayers for the world around us.

"God, help people believe when I share the Gospel with them," is a general invocation we can say, getting more specific as evangelistic needs unfold. Another invocation might be: "God, help people believe the message of the Gospel that other people tell them."

And it doesn't end there; you can get more specific in these prayers, naming names and asking the Lord to crack open even the most closed-off portions of people's hearts.

Jesus very clearly shows us how to begin to spread the Gospel and disciple nations — and it doesn't just stop with your friends, family, or loved ones.

Presidents, senators, congressman, governors, and mayors of our cities can and some will believe in Jesus and be baptized in the name of the Father, Son, and Holy Spirit when we engage in evangelism prayer, the most important method we can activate.

We see the proof of prayer evangelism's power in individual story after story, with people's lives being wholeheartedly transformed.

ANGELINA'S STORY: AN EXAMPLE OF PRAYER EVANGELISM

I've seen again and again in my own life and ministry how prayer is often a conduit to the unexpected.

When we listen to the Holy Spirit, we often find ourselves asking for, experiencing — and receiving — unexpected and incredible things. And when we pray for others, we often see them experience miracles.

I saw a prime example of this paradigm come to fruition when I was in Nuremberg, Germany, in 2014 doing ministry with a friend and his evangelistic organization that was working to spread the gospel overseas.

In an incredible showing of the thirst for the Lord, thousands of people had gathered at a stadium in Nuremberg to hear the Gospel of Christ — a truly stunning sight to see. One afternoon during the weeklong event, the massive horde of attendees flooded out of the stadium and took to the city's streets to share Jesus with passersby.

Having just had a painful back surgery, I decided to hang back and take some time to pray, journal, and reflect inside the now-quieted stadium. During this time of what I assumed would be quiet contemplation, I was absolutely unprepared for what God would do next.

As I was praying and writing, I noticed a small group — two young men and an elderly woman — beginning to approach the area where I was sitting. The unassuming woman, who had a scarf wrapped around her head and appeared to be in her mid-80s, was relatively short; her aging brown hair and brown eyes clearly belonged to someone who had quite a story to share, as I would soon find out.

Despite the massive stadium having 50,000 empty seats, the group inched closer and closer to me. Considering I was just a small speck in the midst of the cleared-out venue, I had a feeling, based on their movements, they were going to directly approach me. Sure enough, the young men very literally sat their elderly grandmother right next to me.

I'll admit I was at first a bit surprised and mildly annoyed by the intrusion. I thought to myself, "I am in an empty stadium and you chose to plop down right next to me in the midst of my prayer and journaling?"

After all, I was in my religious groove as I spent time with the Lord.

But then I quickly came to realize there was an eternal purpose to their decision to come over to me, and I was humbled as I learned the woman's story.

One of her grandchildren broke through the silence, delivering a request that quickly eviscerated any of my remaining qualms: "Would you pray for grand-ma-ma?" In a moment of conviction at my own annoyance — and in the midst of the realization these folks were looking for authentic love and prayer — I asked if they spoke English, to which the German men replied, "Very little."

Then, I asked if they had someone who might be able to help us translate. The young men, who told me their grandma's name was Angelina, immediately set off to find someone who might be able to help.

Before too long, they found a young guy named Lars, a short, humorous, blonde-haired kid who donned a San Francisco Giants baseball cap. As Lars and I sat down to pray with Angelina, she suddenly asked us to pause so she could get something out of her purse.

As her arm moved into her handbag to retrieve an old photograph, I saw something I'll never forget; Angelina had a string of numbers tattooed on the inside of her forearm, a chilling symbol codifying Adolf Hitler's venomous reign of terror.

It was an unmistakable mark from the Holocaust era — a hallmark of the Nazi's vile quest to wipe out and diminish the Jewish people.

Tears began to well up in my eyes. I began to cry, regretting my initial annoyance at their approaching me, and thought, "God, I'm an idiot. Forgive me. Please touch Angelina and her grandchildren."

Meanwhile, Angelina remained resolute as she was now showing us the photograph she had fished out of her purse. The grainy, black-and-white snapshot showed what seemed to be a happy family, with a man and woman smiling and holding an adorable infant.

Of course, photos are mere encapsulations of moments in time and lack any relevant context or back story, which Angelina, in this case, was fully prepared to offer. Just as quickly as I realized she was a survivor of one of history's most horrific atrocities, she began to tell her story — an auditory experience I'll never forget.

She explained, through Lars' astute translations, that the photo had captured her parents holding her as an infant. The happiness in that snapshot was fleeting, though, as Angelina, her mom, and her dad, ended up becoming entrapped in Hitler's horror, later finding themselves in a concentration camp in Austerlitz, Poland.

Angelina then proceeded to explain the truly tragic situation that unfolded at the end of the war. Her family had suffered greatly, but Hitler's reign was coming to an end. The Allies had won the war and defeated Hitler and the English were coming to save the Jews. But Hitler wanted to kill all the Jews before the Allies could reach them, putting the family and everyone else in the camp at grave risk.

Angelina was with her mother in the camp when rumors began to spread that her mom's section would soon be slaughtered. Facing the unthinkable, her mother scrambled to transfer Angelina to her father's bloc in a last-ditch effort to save her baby's life.

Tragically, Angelina's mother was right to make the move, as she was soon murdered along with others in her section.

Despite Angelina being moved to be with her father, the terror was nowhere near over, as he, too, soon received news his section of the camp would be killed. Like Angelina's mother, her dad had to make the painful and incomprehensible decision to separate from his beloved daughter.

But this time, he had to release the child to strangers, transferring Angelina to yet another section of the camp and praying her life would be spared once his own was snuffed out. Angelina's father was, indeed, killed in the gas chambers, leaving her an orphan, yet sparing her from her parents' fate.

I sat transfixed as she explained how her mother's and father's selfless actions and intense love shuffled her about the camp, saving her life again and again until she was eventually rescued by the British.

The photo from her purse — an image offering a glimpse at a once-happy family — was the only remaining artifact she had to recollect the parents the Lord had given her. The sting of her loss and the gravity of the pain were palpable in those moments as the now-elderly woman recounted it all.

With tears in my eyes, I finally honored her grandsons' initial request and uttered a simple prayer for Angelina. I don't fully remember exactly what I prayed, as the experience of hearing her story left me in emotional tatters.

I do remember it was just a simple prayer, not much longer than a few minutes. When I finished praying, Angelina and her grandsons thanked me. As I said goodbye, I didn't realize it would be the only conversation I'd ever have with the Holocaust survivor.

Later that night, though, during worship inside the stadium, I was fortunate to meet Angelina's entire family. While she didn't personally attend that gathering, 19 of her family members — including her daughters and grandchildren — came up to me and revealed something absolutely incredible: Jesus touched Angelina that day.

While Angelina had very likely heard the Gospel many times before through her own family members, somehow our interaction and that simple prayer was the final piece of the puzzle she needed to connect all of the dots.

As I ponder my interaction with Angelina, I'm reminded we can never truly know what's unfolding inside a person's heart and mind.

That's why we must follow 1 Peter 3:15 which tells us to always be ready to give an answer to every person who asks us for the hope we have.

We can be assured that when we pray, it is the power and mystery of the Holy Spirit who touches people and reveals Jesus to them.

This is why we must trust, obey, and pray without ceasing — even when we're not fully sure what to say or when we feel our prayerful words simply aren't all that profound.

I was initially reluctant that day to be bothered by Angelina and her family, focusing on my own goals and ambitions. I'm now deeply fortunate and grateful the Lord is merciful, though, and still used me as He saw fit, pushing to the side my own selfish desires to take a brief moment to pray with a woman who desperately needed it.

As it turns out, Angelina's family members were Messianic Jews who had come to embrace Christ as their Lord and Savior. In fact, her oldest daughter had become a pastor. I can only imagine the suffering and rejection they must have lived through.

That night, in the midst of that crowded stadium filled with thousands of men and women worshiping Jesus, Angelina's daughter, the pastor, asked, "Are you the man who prayed for my mother?" When I responded affirmatively, she teared up, gave me a giant hug, and kissed me on both cheeks — and the other family members followed suit.

Their gratitude was overwhelming, as I learned that my simple prayer earlier in the day had a profound impact on Angelina, helping to heal her heart and break through past trauma. She was now, like her family members, able to believe in Jesus as the Savior of Israel — something she hadn't yet done before that day.

With Jesus Culture beautifully filling the stadium with worship music, I watched in awe as Angelina's family lifted their hands in the air and my heart filled with gratitude, pondering what the Holy Spirit had done that day through a simple prayer.

The prayer was so uncomplicated I wouldn't have thought anything more about it had I not met Angelina's family that night. There was no call to salvation, no prophetic word, no major moment; it was a benign act of love for Angelina and an honoring of her grandsons' request — nothing more.

Yet the simplicity of that prayer shows the power of the Holy Spirit to reach hearts when we trust God and live out prayerful lives as He commands. In this case, God worked through even my reluctant obedience. It was the completion of just one of the billions of eternal tapestries the Lord so brilliantly weaves together each and every day.

And that's how the God works. The simplicity of prayer evangelism is waiting for God to reveal Jesus to the lost. We often assume we must utter large, deep, boisterous prayers in order for the Lord to work, but we err when we assume we're the ones with the ability to do the work of changing hearts.

As believers, we're called to be persistent and to trust and obey. My prayer for Angelina wasn't anything special, yet the Lord used it as the final blow to crack open her heart to his love. It's through steady faith that prayer evangelism makes all the difference.

THE ESSENTIAL INGREDIENTS OF PRAYER EVANGELISM

We see again and again in Scripture what happens when people truly turn to prayer and reliance on the Lord. It all begins with trust and obedience, with a recognition that prayer evangelism changes things.

The world today is reeling in pain as many reject the truth and seek to satisfy themselves. And while that dynamic isn't new, neither is the solution: Jesus. It's quite easy to look around us and feel discouraged, though the confusion and pain others feel should motivate us to move deeper into prayer evangelism for our friends, loved ones, communities, cultures, and nation.

2 Corinthians 4 (KJV) reminds us of what's bubbling beneath the surface, with Paul writing that Christians have "renounced the hidden things of dishonesty, not walking in craftiness, nor handling the word of God deceitfully; but by manifestation of the truth commending ourselves to every man's conscience in the sight of God" (verse 2).

But Paul also juxtaposes the Christian experience to the lack of understanding for those who "are lost," explaining how Satan has blinded these individuals to truth.

"In whom the god of this world hath blinded the minds of them which believe not, lest the light of the glorious gospel of Christ, who is the image of God, should shine unto them," verse 4 reads, with the subsequent Scripture reading, "For we preach not ourselves, but Christ Jesus the Lord; and ourselves your servants for Jesus' sake."

We must engage in prayer evangelism and seek the Lord on behalf of those who are blinded and who desperately need Him. This ranges from specific prayers for changed hearts and minds to humbly sitting down with people like Angelina to seek God's blessing over their lives.

The situations and circumstances surrounding prayer evangelism won't always look the same, but the consistent component is always belief — a confidence in God's promises and a commitment to live out the Lord's love.

And that's what I absolutely love about my interaction with Angelina. Who would have ever believed that the prayers, tears, and hopes of many over a long time would combine with one simple prayer from an admittedly reluctant pastor in a near-empty stadium through a translator named Lars to win over the heart of a beleaguered Holocaust survivor?

And it all happened in Nuremberg, Germany, where Hitler's Nazism and reign of terror once raged. This former bastion of evil would become the very place where Angelina would be saved, with a simple prayer that finally helped open her eyes.

That night was the last time I ever spoke with anyone from Angelina's family, but I'll truly never forget the experience, as it taught me a valuable lesson about prayer evangelism.

Some of us are called to plant, and some to water, but God is responsible for the growth.

And that's why I come back to our essential ingredients for successful prayer evangelism: trusting, obeying, and praying. Rather than obsessing over the end result, we must seek God and place the burdens in His hands.

As I sat inside the stadium that night, I wasn't only struck by Angelina's story and her incredible family; I was also taken by the gravity of the scene before me.

A group of Messianic Jews and Christians were worshipping together, holding up the German and Israeli flags in unison — symbols that just decades before no one could have ever imagined seeing coalesce.

Yet there, on the very spot where Hitler launched Nazism, the result of so many prayers over the decades was on full display. There's no doubt many assumed Nuremberg could never be converted and that Jews wouldn't ever be safe there again.

But there we all were, with the Israeli and German flags waving together and the results of prayer evangelism coming to fruition in such a beautiful way.

It all pointed to a God who does immeasurably more than we could ever ask and imagine — and to our need to stay the course as we trust, pray, and obey.

PRESENCE EVANGELISM

"THOU SHALT LOVE the Lord thy God with all thy heart, and with all thy soul, and with all thy mind. This is the first and great commandment," Jesus proclaims in Matthew 22:37-38 (KJV), with verses 39-40 continuing, "And the second is like unto it, Thou shalt love thy neighbour as thyself. On these two commandments hang all the law and the prophets."

Jesus' recipe for "loving God" and "loving others" offers powerful guidance for His followers as they seek to live out the Lord's commands. For the purposes of this next chapter, we'll explore a type of evangelism that falls under the category of the latter.

Presence evangelism is simply the presence of God in your life when it comes to forming a relationship. It's displaying the kindness of God to others — a goodness that sets a godly example and leads to repentance.

Much of presence evangelism involves a love for others that manifests itself through good deeds and compassionate acts. And this sort of relational kindness should start from the moment a believer first meets someone.

In those initial reactions, he or she is called to be respectful and altruistic, taking time to ask another person about themselves and learn more about the individual. We must always remember Christ is in us and we operate through the Holy Spirit! His presence touches people even if we don't feel it. He is always working when we are reaching out to people.

When this posture carries from the beginning of a friendship or relationship throughout its lifecycle, Christians have real and consistent opportunities to show people God's love in the way they selflessly approach various aspects of the relationship.

"Loving our neighbor" can be simple and can be exemplified in a variety of ways. It's been said that "a good deed creates a good mood to open the door for the good news." And when we love our neighbors as ourselves, we open pathways for the Gospel to inspire others and pique their interest in what it truly means to be a Christ-follower.

The radical nature of Jesus' words and behaviors shouldn't be lost on us, particularly when it comes to our enemies. It's easy to love our friends and those we like, but what about our foes — what about the people who have gone out of their way to hurt or harm us?

God calls us to show the same love and to engage in presence evangelism even with these folks. "If you're enemy is hungry, feed him"[71] (Romans 12:20, NIV) and "Pray for those who persecute you"[72] (Matthew 5:44, NIV) are perhaps the most extreme forms of caring for one's neighbor.

And there's a powerful reality in these shocking calls embedded in God's instructions to us: living out these proclamations helps us win people over with our good deeds — all while showing, at moments, an otherworldly love and compassion so profound it shocks people into wondering, "What in the world is different about that person?"

That difference, of course, is Christ. And once that's recognized, the sky truly is the limit.

As the Apostle Paul so astutely reminds us, "Don't you know it is God's kindness that leads us to repentance?" (Romans 2:4). In other words, when you finally believe a person loves you, you might be open to the love that drives their heart for you.

When it comes to presence evangelism, there are some simple and

71 Bible Gateway. "Romans 12:20, New International Version." Bible Gateway. Accessed February 9, 2025. https://www.biblegateway.com/passage/?search=Romans+12%3A20&version=NIV.
72 Bible Gateway, "Matthew 5:44, New International Version," Bible Gateway, accessed February 9, 2025, https://www.biblegateway.com/passage/?search=Matthew+5%3A44&version=NIV.

important examples we can look to as we seek to understand how it works and where we err in living it out.

THE BONES OF PRESENCE EVANGELISM

It's easy to *talk* about presence evangelism, but what does it really look like to live it out? Believe it or not, there are simple and easy steps and actions we can take today to more profoundly and easily exemplify and embody this form of evangelism.

Perhaps one of the simplest acts is to appropriately tip a waiter or waitress. When you're witnessing to a server, one of the worst things you could ever do is not to tip him or her well. I've seen many Christians simply opt to be cheap in this arena — and it matters.

In fact, it's one of the most offensive things that serves to nullify one's witness to the Gospel message when a believer tells someone about Jesus and then doesn't tip them. In addition to cheapskatery, it completely preaches offense and selfishness.

We can always understand this about evangelism: it is better to give than to receive — and the gift opens the way for the giver. This might seem like strange advice, or ill-fitted considering this is a book about evangelism. But just bear with me, because the impact can be profound.

I know a group of Christians from a local house church who became aware of a single mom who waitressed at a diner and they decided to take action; they came together and tipped the woman a whopping $3,000. If we're honest, that sum would be enough to raise anyone's eyebrows, which was certainly the case in this scenario.

In fact, the sum was so moving, it became easy for the group to lead the woman to Christ! It's a prime example of the gift opening the way for the giver. Now, I know what you're thinking: "I don't have $3,000!" And that's OK; most people don't.

But that doesn't mean you can't take steps to tip well or grab someone's attention by leading with a generous and compassionate heart. It doesn't even have to be a waitress. Consider paying it forward by covering a meal or coffee for the person behind you, or even offering to carry someone's bags to their car at the grocery store.

When it comes to presence evangelism, these simple steps can go a long way.

There are plenty of other examples of how this type of evangelism can play itself out. Toys for Tots — an annual effort to collect toys for children whose parents cannot afford them — and other similar efforts offer a profound and simple holiday-time effort to express love for others.

There is nothing more fun or illuminating than igniting a kid's world by giving them a Christmas present. What greater example do we need than Nicholas of Myra a.k.a. St. Nicholas 270-343 A.D. who changed the world with presence evangelism? The fact remains: one of the most fun and easiest ways to share the birth of Christ is to give gifts to people — just like the Wise Men did when they finally reached Jesus.

Evangelism is just that: bearing gifts in the name of Christ.

Or, how about finding out if there are local kids in need of school supplies at the start of the school year (or throughout)? It's easy to reach out to local schools, especially if you have kids or grandkids who attend.

One of the best ways to live out presence evangelism is when neighbors step in to help fellow neighbors. In that vein, you could also host a party or neighborhood cookout, a chance to invite people to your home to feast — and fellowship. What better way to share the Gospel than by providing food and fun, which, in turn, can yield Gospel conversations?

You've heard it is said that "sharing is caring," and that's a statement by which the early church truly lived. In the Book of Acts, we see a church that had everything in common; no one had needs, and, thus, they had favor with the entire city.

"And the multitude of them that believed were of one heart and of one soul," Acts 4:32 (KJV) reads. "Neither said any of them that ought of the things which he possessed was his own; but they had all things common."

We see in these verses how early believers put together their resources to distribute to people based on their needs — a powerful example for us to follow as we seek to live out a range of activities that fall under the umbrella of presence evangelism.

We see James offer some stirring words about what it means to truly follow Jesus, sacrificing and caring for some of the most vulnerable.

"Pure religion and undefiled before God and the Father is this: to visit the fatherless and widows in their affliction, and to keep himself unspotted from the world," he wrote (James 1:27, KJV).

And Jesus Himself further illuminates these concepts in Matthew 25 while speaking about the "sheep and the goats," expressing the importance of living out presence evangelism. After Christ's return, the Lord will speak to the sheep and offer an "inheritance," expressing the devotion to Him — and the love and compassion — through which they lived.

"For I was hungry and you gave me something to eat, I was thirsty and you gave me something to drink, I was a stranger and you invited me in, I needed clothes and you clothed me, I was sick and you looked after me, I was in prison and you came to visit me," Jesus proclaims in Matthew 25:35-36 (NIV).

God then says in Matthew 25:40 what one of these sheep has done to the "least of these" they have done to Him, offering a powerful image of the love for others He expects of His followers. The most stunning indictment, of course, comes when the Lord speaks to those "goats" who did not live out their call to show compassion and love for others.

"Then he will say to those on his left, 'Depart from me, you who are cursed, into the eternal fire prepared for the devil and his angels," verse 41 (NIV) reads, with the subsequent text in verses 42-43 continuing: "For I was hungry and you gave me nothing to eat, I was thirsty and you gave me nothing to drink, I was a stranger and you did not invite me in, I needed clothes and you did not clothe me, I was sick and in prison and you did not look after me.'"

These verses are a reminder that the call to love others — to show up with acts of presence evangelism — isn't merely a willy-nilly option we can engage in if we so choose; it's an expectation that illustrates the depths to which we've allowed the Gospel to permeate our hearts.

When I think about feeding the poor, in particular, one person specifically comes to mind — Mother Teresa. Her heart to feed the poor and to help those in poverty inspired the entire world. Her dedication to obeying God's Commission to feed the poor showed that serving the least of these can help make Christ known to the nations.

The late humanitarian once said, "If you can't feed a hundred people, then feed just one."[73] We often become so consumed with reaching the many that we forget the importance of individually ministering to each individual heart.

CORPORATE PRESENCE EVANGELISM

Much of presence evangelism involves a one-on-one connection that draws people closer to God's love. But this type of evangelism also comes in another form: a believer or cohort of Christians coming together to create systems, organizations, or movements that serve others in an effort to meet needs and, in turn, create a vertical connection to the Lord.

Christian gatherings, book clubs, meetings, support groups — and even churches themselves — become the central locations where people can be spiritually nourished. And when you go to evangelize a city and make a disciple of it, these places for believers to gather and reach out to the community become absolutely essential.

In the Scriptures, these hubs for the spread of the Gospel took on differing forms. Many times, early believers met in one another's homes. This is often the case today, with so-called "house churches" bringing together small groups of Christians.

Often, these meetings grow and, over time, there are enough believers in a community to build a church or a facility to accommodate the growing assembly. Churches are essential to all types of evangelism, as they're the locations where people go to learn, develop, and tend to the spiritual seeds that have been planted.

There's power in numbers, particularly when people are assembled together in the Lord's name. Jesus proclaims as much in Matthew 18:20 (KJV): "For where two or three are gathered together in my name, there am I in the midst of them."

---

73 Mother Teresa, "If you can't feed a hundred people, then feed just one," Goodreads, accessed February 9, 2025, https://www.goodreads.com/quotes/9181130-if-you-can-t-feed-a-hundred-people-then-feed-just.

Thus, the role of churches — healthy, Bible-believing, Christ-honoring, Gospel-centric houses of worship — is essential in the evangelistic ecosystem. To evangelize a city, state, or town, we must have churches or strategic places for believers to meet and function in unity.

This is essential not only to the spiritual health of individual believers, but to the building of strategy, passion, and ability to reach other people in the community for Christ.

The Spirit of God seeks to unify churches to work together instead of obsessively being divided over doctrine so that the good news can be preached to all the world. Unfortunately, many churches miss out on collaborative presence evangelism opportunities due to these differences.

Yet one area where this is lived out well by many Christians and churches is in nonprofit ministries, particularly those that specialize in disaster relief. There are many examples of these Christian organizations, with some taking a general Christian posture — an interdenominational force with the ability to make a massive impact on the Kingdom.

Operation Blessing is one such organization that was founded with the sole intent of disaster relief. The humanitarian organization's official description expresses its desire to partner with supporters to "demonstrate God's love by alleviating human suffering in the U.S. and around the world" and to "truly be the hands and feet of Jesus for those who are suffering and in need."[74]

When hurricanes, earthquakes, tornadoes, or forest fires break out, the ministry immediately mobilizes to send semi-trucks full of food, clothing, sleeping cots, and supplies to help the victims. The Kingdom of Christ shines brightly in these areas because groups like Operation Blessing have a united belief in helping in the name of Jesus.

We see in Scripture that Luke was a physician. Undoubtedly, part of evangelism is healing the sick — in mind, body, spirit, and soul. It's wonderful to give a tip to a waitress or to find other ways to show up to live out presence evangelism. But one structural way this has been

---

74 Operation Blessing, "What We Do," Operation Blessing, accessed February 9, 2025, https://www.ob.org/what-we-do/.

fulfilled in a bigger, broader sense is through the creation of massive institutions like hospitals. Building medical facilities is one of the things the Catholic Church has done well in serving to advance the Kingdom of God.

They have raised millions of dollars to build hospitals, many times constructing them in honor of Christians who have helped take care of the sick. Take a moment to ponder the millions of lives that have been saved by hospitals and the temporal — and eternal — impact these facilities have had.

The truth is: If a person is not alive, it is impossible for them to be saved. A man is appointed once to die and then comes the judgment. Life is a gift, and corporate presence evangelism in the form of Christian ministries and hospitals has helped to sustain so many.

Another similar area for Christians to consider is the impact of schools in the community. We spend a lot of time speaking about the need to evangelize the next generation, yet we often forget that one of the biggest networks in almost every community is the school system.

Where else can you find the entire younger generation concentrated in one place but in schools? When you have favor with your local schools — public, charter, and private — it creates open doors to share the good news of the Gospel.

The Bible is clear about our mandate to raise children with a love for truth and the Lord. Proverbs 22:6 (KJV) reads, "Train up a child in the way he should go: And when he is old, he will not depart from it."

It's no secret some schools struggle with Woke and gender ideology and other mixed messages that create barriers to instilling wisdom and truth. Dealing with those issues in their entirety is perhaps a separate book — or even a volume of texts — but there are some basic realities we must confront.

First and foremost, millions of children are in the public school system, and, at its core, education intends to teach kids the skills they need to advance in life, eventually, get a job, and earn income. Thus, schools are important as central gathering places.

Regardless of where people land on sending their children (homeschool, public, private, or the like), it's essential to look for ways to have a presence in and around educational facilities, extending oneself in these core communities through presence evangelism.

Another area where this is important is in the church planting realm. In fact, creating new places of worship is one of the most natural examples of presence evangelism. Placing a new church in a community that doesn't have one makes God's presence known to that community or neighborhood in the most amazing of ways.

As we conclude our look at presence evangelism, we can examine a few powerful examples of Jesus engaging in this manner. While these instances rely on the miraculous and can't precisely be replicated by human hearts and minds, they serve as a blueprint for the types of evangelistic outreach we can do by being present and showing up to love others.

One of the most compelling examples comes in John 2:1-12, where we see Christ's first miracle unfold — the turning of water into wine at the wedding in Cana of Galilee. Jesus, His disciples, and His mother, Mary, are all present at this marriage banquet when the unthinkable happens: the wedding hosts run out of wine.

Mary, Jesus' mom, tells her Son, the wedding hosts "have no wine" (verse 3), to which He initially pushes back and proclaims His hour "hasn't come yet" (verse 4). We don't know all the details of what happened next to push Jesus to inevitably help out, but we see His mother tell the servants to listen to whatever Jesus tells them to do.

So, the servants fill jugs to the brim with water, which Christ then turned into wine — and not just any wine. John 2:9-10 tells us that the "ruler of the feast" tasted Jesus' water turned to wine and determined it was much better than what was initially served during the feast.

"Every man at the beginning sets forth good wine, and when men have well drunk, he then serves up that which is worse," the banquet master essentially said. "But you kept the good wine until now."

The Bible doesn't go into great detail about *why* Jesus chose to perform this first public miracle — an act that had nothing to do with healing the sick, expelling demons, or acting in a way to combat the physical or spiritual realms.

I believe Jesus' decision to perform this miracle was based on Him showing up, being present, and seeing to it that people had a good time during an important wedding celebration. There are certainly different ideas and theories as to the "why," but we can conclude a number of realities based on the miracle itself.

In John 2:11 (KJV), we're told the miracle "manifested forth his glory" and that "his disciples believed in him." So, while it appears to be a relatively benign act in itself, creating wine from water had a profound impact in showcasing Jesus' power and sparking belief in Him.

In a thoughtful article on the matter, Danielle Bernock wrote the following on Christianity.com:

> Changing water into wine requires demonstrating power over time and space. Wine requires many processes that cover a long period of time. The growth of the plant. The maturation of the grape. Harvesting the grape. Treading the grapes into juice. The aging time required for fermentation. Great wine takes a long time to ferment. Jesus bypassed the entire timeframe in moments, which only God can do.[75]

This shouldn't be lost on the reader. There's another consideration as well, though, and it surrounds the reasons why Jesus might have chosen to engage in this act of presence evangelism: family honor.

In the cultural context of the time, weddings usually lasted a week, a time during which food and wine were offered by the hosting families. As GotQuestions.org notes, "To run out of either implied a thoughtless or impoverished host" and to have no wine left to give would "bring dishonor upon the family name."[76]

While we don't have all of the context in the biblical text, this could be another reason Christ chose to show up in such a compelling, gentle, yet influential way.

Another example we see in Scripture is Jesus feeding hordes of people, a miraculous model of presence evangelism. In Matthew

---

75 Danielle Bernock, "Why Did Jesus Turn Water into Wine?" Christianity.com, October 12, 2023, accessed February 9, 2025, https://www.christianity.com/wiki/jesus-christ/why-did-jesus-turn-water-into-wine.html.
76 GotQuestions.org, "Why Did Jesus Choose the Wedding at Cana for His First Miracle?" GotQuestions.org, accessed February 9, 2025, https://www.gotquestions.org/wedding-at-Cana.html.

15:32-39 and Mark 8:1-10, we see Jesus supernaturally taking very little food — seven loaves of bread and a few fish, to be precise — and feeding 4,000 people.

The Bible tells us great crowds had coalesced to bring Him the blind, crippled, and mute, with Christ compassionately healing these folks. The people were amazed — but they were also hungry, having been with Jesus for days and in need of sustenance.

Recognizing they had quite the conundrum considering the need for food and the crowd size, the disciples essentially asked Jesus: Where in the world would we get enough bread in the midst of a wilderness to feed this massive crowd?

They, of course, failed at that moment to recognize what Jesus' presence meant — that anything was possible, even the feeding of 4,000 with just a few loaves of bread and some tiny fish.

As we can see, Jesus meets the needs of those in the crowd by commanding them to sit on the ground, giving thanks, breaking the fish and bread up, and passing it out. The Bible tells us the 4,000 "did all eat, and were filled" (Matthew 15:37, KJV).

And not only that but there was enough left over to fill seven baskets. What's even more remarkable is that Jesus did this again in the Bible when He fed an even larger crowd of 5,000.

There are a lot of lessons here and much theological conversation to be had about these miraculous acts, but for the purposes of this chapter, there's a powerful reality when it comes to presence evangelism: Jesus saw a need, He showed up, and He met it.

Part of achieving the King's Gambit is relying on the smallest of good deeds through the power and mystery of the Holy Spirit. That's when we see the miraculous happen. Tipping a waitress holds the power to help lead her to salvation and prayer can spark miraculous healings in hospitals.

The sky is the limit when it comes to the Lord, and these engagements hold the power — by just showing up — to change everything.

God's power today is just as real and will increase as we approach His return. When we see needs, we must trust, pray, and meet them, living out presence evangelism in the process and trusting Lord to do the rest.

PRESENTATION EVANGELISM

⟿

IN ADDITION TO prayer and presence evangelism comes another type of Gospel-sharing — something we call presentation evangelism. This is exactly what it sounds like; it places a strong emphasis on clearly sharing and communicating the central beliefs of Christianity and Scripture in a structured and cohesive manner.

Our first two evangelistic models focused on actions surrounding an appeal to God and meeting people's needs; this third form takes our ability to share the Truth in a compelling way that helps drive home Jesus' message.

One of the most well-known modes through which the Gospel is shared is by pastors from the pulpit. The word "preaching" comes from the Greek word "kerygma" which means "to share the gospel or the good news."

In Christian theology, this refers to "oral instruction" and "refers primarily to the preaching of the Apostles as recorded in the New Testament," according to Britannica.[77] But presentation evangelism isn't just about pastors sharing biblical truth in the sanctuary; it's about each of us being prepared to share the Truth with others.

Presentation evangelism is an opportunity — a potentially soul-saving moment when the door is open for you to tell someone

---

77 Encyclopedia Britannica. "Kerygma and Catechesis." Encyclopædia Britannica. Accessed February 9, 2025. https://www.britannica.com/topic/kerygma.

how to receive the Holy Spirit. The Bible tells us, "If you confess with your mouth that Jesus is Lord and believe in your heart that God raised him from the dead, you will be saved" (Romans 10:9, ESV).

We see Jesus affirm this message in His powerful conversation with Nicodemus, a Pharisee who visits Christ with some essential, pertinent questions. John 3 is perhaps one of the most well-known examples of Jesus' presentation evangelism taking form.

In this portion of Scripture, Nicodemus comes to Jesus at night and essentially starts by telling Christ he believes Jesus is a teacher from God because "no man can do these miracles" unless the Lord is with him.

Jesus' response is fascinating: "Verily, verily, I say unto you, except a man be born again, he cannot see the kingdom of God" (John 3:3, amended KJV). And this is where the conversation gets quite interesting.

Here's a transcript boiling down where their chat goes from there:

Nicodemus: How can a man be born when he is old? Can he enter the second time into his mother's womb, and be born?

> **Jesus:** Verily, verily, I say unto thee, except a man be born of water and of the Spirit, he cannot enter into the kingdom of God. That which is born of the flesh is flesh; and that which is born of the Spirit is spirit. … You must be born again.

Nicodemus: How can these things be?

Jesus: Aren't you a master of Israel, and don't know these things? Verily, verily, I say

> unto thee, we speak that we do know, and testify that we have seen; and you receive not our witness. If I have told you earthly things, and you believe not, how shall you believe if I tell you of heavenly things? And no man hath ascended up to heaven, but he that came down from heaven, even the Son of man which is in heaven. And as Moses lifted up the serpent in the wilderness, even so must the Son of man be lifted up: That whosoever believes in him should not perish, but have eternal life. For God so loved the world, that he gave his only begotten

> Son, that whosoever believes in him should not perish, but
> have everlasting life. For God sent not his Son into the world
> to condemn the world; but that the world through him might
> be saved. He that believeth on him is not condemned: but he
> that believeth not is condemned already, because he hath not
> believed in the name of the only begotten Son of God.

Jesus goes on to note that, with His coming, "light has come into
the world," though men have loved darkness more than light.

He offers a clear presentation of the need to rely on Him to reach
God and attain salvation; it's the very message He calls His disciples
— and all of us to — with His revelation of the Great Commission in
Matthew 28:16-20.

Christ proclaims, "Go and teach all nations, baptizing them in the
name of the Father, and of the Son, and of the Holy Ghost."

When it comes to the evangelism model, the presentation piece
of the puzzle can sometimes create barriers, as some people become
nervous or uncertain of how to formulate the message or practically
deliver it.

It's one thing to pray and be present; it's another to formulate and
deliver a message. And yet we see Jesus' balance of truth and love played
out throughout Scripture, offering a model for how we can progress.

We also see these patterns with the Apostle Paul. In fact, the
Book of Romans is one of the greatest revelations on salvation and
its complete presentation. Some ministries have used the text to
formulate a simplified salvation message known as the "Romans Road
to Salvation."

It's essentially a Gospel breakdown using verses from Romans,
guiding people through their need for Jesus, His sacrifice, and what it all
means to heal the human condition. Let's revisit the earlier breakdown
of the "Romans Road":

- We are all sinners and must be saved by the sacrifice and
  payment of Christ. All have sinned and fallen short of the glory
  of God. (Romans 3:9-12)
- The wages of sin is death. (Romans 6:23)

- God shows his love for us for why we were still sinners Christ died for us. (Romans 5:8)
- The promise of eternal life. (Romans 10:9-13)
- We have been made righteous through what Christ has done. (Romans 5:1;8:38-39)
- Nothing can separate us from the love of Christ.

This certainly gives us a model we can use to share the Gospel in a comprehensive and moving way, though there are some tips we must take into account when it comes to properly living out presentation evangelism.

We see countless organizations working in the U.S. and around the globe that center the entirety of their mission on presentation evangelism, conjuring up creative tactics to reach people with biblical truth.

Cru, formerly known as Campus Crusade for Christ, was founded in 1951 by Bill and Vonette Bright at the University of California, Los Angeles, campus. That simple act sparked a massive organization that has spanned decades and touched people across the globe.

In 2020, Cru reported having 19,000 staff members in over 190 countries, offering "spiritual guidance, resources, and programs tailored for people from all cultures in every walk of life."[78]

Throughout the years Cru has worked in arenas such as poverty alleviation and apologetics, but one of the most well-known presentation tools created in history was Bright's "Have You Heard of the Four Spiritual Laws?" According to Cru, with 2.5 billion printed, it very well could be the "most widely distributed religious booklet in history."[79]

This simple Gospel breakdown has remained incredibly powerful due to its simple explanation of Jesus' life, love, and significance.

"What does it take to begin a relationship with God? Devote yourself to unselfish religious deeds? Become a better person so that God will accept you?" Cru writes in an explanation. "You may be

---

78 Cru, "Cru Historical Fact Sheet," Cru, accessed February 9, 2025, https://www.cru.org/us/en/about/cru-press/background/cru-historical-fact-sheet.html.
79 Cru, "Cru Historical Fact Sheet."

surprised that none of those things will work. But God has made it very clear in the Bible how we can know Him."[80]

The "Four Spiritual Laws," thus, offer guidance on how to start a relationship with Jesus. While there's much to break down in each of the laws, Bright formulated them as follows:

1. Law One: "God loves you and offers a wonderful plan for your life."

2. Law Two: "All of us sin and our sin has separated us from God."

3. Law Three: "Jesus Christ is God's only provision for our sin. Through Him we can know and experience God's love and plan for our life."

4. Law Four: "We must individually receive Jesus Christ as Savior and Lord; then we can know and experience God's love and plan for our lives."[81]

This, of course, is just one of the other presentation evangelism tools available to believers looking for expressive and accurate ways to share the Christian message with others.

As we ponder the full scope of presentation evangelism, we'd be remiss to overlook some of the most powerful communicators of the Gospel we've seen in the modern era.

Without a doubt, the late Billy Graham is most known for traversing the world with the Christian message. Graham, who died in 2018 at the age of 99, is very literally the poster child for presentation evangelism.

"We must warn the nations of the world that they must repent and turn to God while there is yet time," the evangelist once said. "We must also proclaim that there is forgiveness and peace in knowing Jesus Christ as Savior and Lord."[82]

And Graham lived out this message. In America — and internationally — he preached the Gospel through the scriptures to stadiums

---

80 Cru. "Would You Like to Know God Personally?" Cru. Accessed February 9, 2025. https://www.cru.org/ph/en/how-to-know-god/would-you-like-to-know-god-personally1.html.
81 Cru, "Would You Like to Know God Personally?"
82 Billy Graham Library, "10 Quotes from Billy Graham on World Evangelism," Billy Graham Library, April 10, 2022, accessed February 9, 2025, https://billygrahamlibrary.org/blog-10-quotes-from-billy-graham-on-world-evangelism/.

filled with thousands of people who came to hear him preach and gave their lives to Christ. These events, known as "crusades," changed millions of lives.

He also started the Billy Graham Evangelistic Association, which taught believers how to spread the Gospel; that organization continues its work on the ground and even online, furthering the mission of its founder well after his death.

Graham's evangelism influence was so powerful he was often called in to counsel U.S. presidents. In fact, Graham met with presidents from Harry Truman to Barack Obama — and met with Donald Trump before he ran for president in 2016.[83]

What made Graham so unique was the viral nature of his ministry well before there was a Facebook, Twitter, or TikTok. He became a household name due to his penchant for presentation evangelism and had a knack for seeing through new and innovative pathways to spread the Gospel.

"All over the world, God is opening doors of opportunity, making it possible for us to take the Gospel to millions who have never heard of Christ," he once said.[84]

And those doors remain open, while new ones emerge with the increase and growth of technology and new capabilities.

In addition to preaching the Gospel, apologetics is another form of presentation evangelism. Defined by GotQuestions.org as "the science of giving a defense of the Christian faith," this form of sharing focuses on responding to skepticism and attack on belief.[85]

But it also lends itself to equipping believers to be prepared to meet those objections, to know the reasons they believe biblical truth, and to respond to false teachers in the church who might be perverting the Gospel message.

In the end, apologetics is about offering hope — and defining and

---

83 ABC News, "Rev. Billy Graham Counseled President Truman," ABC News, May 12, 2011, accessed February 9, 2025, https://abcnews.go.com/Politics/rev-billy-graham-counseled-president-truman/story?id=13583583.

84 Billy Graham Library, "10 Quotes from Billy Graham on World Evangelism."

85 GotQuestions.org, "What Is Christian Apologetics?" GotQuestions.org, accessed February 9, 2025, https://www.gotquestions.org/Christian-apologetics.html.

defending the reasons for it. Josh McDowell is by far one of the most well-known Christians to advance this arena.

He's the head of a Cru ministry in his name and has written some of the most famous apologetic works in the body of Christ to this day, including "Evidence That Demands a Verdict," a book widely heralded for providing evidence to back the Scriptures.

With more than 50 years of ministry behind him, McDowell has spoken to more than 46 million people in 139 countries — and has authored 155 books.[86] His legacy is quite inspiring, and he's joined by others like Lee Strobel, an atheist journalist-turned-Christian author who penned "A Case For Christ," a seminal book showcasing how Strobel went from skeptic to believer.

Strobel has also gone on to write a plethora of additional books dealing with presenting the Gospel, diving into evidence for the Bible, and equipping Christians to answer tough questions.

"I think it's incumbent on Christians to … always be prepared to give an answer to anyone who asks us to give the reason for the hope that we have and to do it gently and respectfully," Strobel told CBN News in a 2023 interview, going on to explain that the evidence for the Gospel is clear and present. "One thing that cannot be said by anybody legitimately is, 'There is no evidence for God.'"[87]

He continued, "You can say, 'I don't believe the evidence.' You can say, 'I reject that evidence.' You can say, 'I'm smarter than that evidence,' but we can't say that there is no evidence."[88]

I have only mentioned a few names on the presentation evangelism front, though history is filled with people who have followed Christ's call and example to share the Gospel in compelling ways.

C.S. Lewis is perhaps the most influential Christian writer of the past 100 years, offering various defenses and explanations of the Gospel through both fiction and nonfiction writings. His book, "Mere

---

86 Josh.org, "Media Information," Josh.org, accessed February 9, 2025, https://www.josh.org/about/media-information/.
87   Billy Hallowell, "'Is God Real?': Famed Author Lee Strobel Explores Proof of God and the Bible," Faithwire, November 14, 2023, accessed February 9, 2025, https://www.faithwire.com/2023/11/14/is-god-real-famed-author-lee-strobel-explores-proof-of-god-and-the-bible/.
88   Hallowell, "'Is God Real?'"

Christianity" is a seminal classic with the power to reach the seemingly unreached.

"C.S. Lewis is the ideal persuader for the half-convinced, for the good man who would like to be a Christian but finds his intellect getting in the way," the late Anthony Burgess of the New York Times Book Review once said.[89]

Some have even said the book is more popular today than when it was first released in 1952 — a notable feat[90]. But considering it's a clear and concise example of presentation evangelism, it should come as no surprise that its reliance on truth has made it resonate.

One essential reality we must recognize, of course, as we talk about people like Graham, Strobel, McDowell, Lewis, and others is that most people engaging in presentation evangelism will never write a book or even publish a website.

Some, like Charles Finney — the father of modern-day revivalism — was reportedly so full of the Holy Spirit that people would come under conviction without him saying anything and they would remarkably ask, "What must I do to be saved?" Finney would simply present the Gospel.

And this speaks to an important caveat when addressing presentation evangelism, and it's a central key to the King's Gambit: the secret to personal evangelism is to be full of the Holy Spirit while having the faith to know the presentation of the Gospel is an expectancy to see the supernatural happen.

The most powerful moments of sharing Jesus in this way unfold during one-on-one conversations. These well-known examples point us toward potential blueprints to follow, though the best example, as noted, is Jesus' conversation with Nicodemus in John 3.

TARGETED PRESENTATION EVANGELISM

One of the most powerful manifestations of presentation evangelism today comes in the form of media outlets geared toward presenting

---

89 C.S. Lewis, Mere Christianity (New York: HarperOne, 2001).
90 George Marsden, "A Biography of Mere Christianity," C.S. Lewis Institute, March 7, 2017, accessed February 9, 2025, https://www.cslewisinstitute.org/resources/a-biography-of-mere-christianity/.

news and current events through a Christian lens. Some outlets take the news approach while others simply create tailored websites that present the Gospel through tackling important life issues.

Regardless of what form it takes, more than ever, we see the spread of biblical truth presented through different forms of media — and it continues to grow and evolve.

Radio preaching persists, though it has morphed in some circles to the Christian podcasting realm, with some turning to social media to engage in presentation evangelism. These sermons and topical podcasts and videos often confront issues head-on.

That said, another form of presentation evangelism has been growing and evolving in the faith space: entertainment evangelism. Companies like Pure Flix (now known as Great American Pure Flix) were founded to create content that inspires Christians while also attempting to bring nonbelievers into the biblical fold.

The company made a major splash in 2014 with the release of "God's Not Dead," a faith-affirming film that went on to gross more than $60 million at the box office.

Great American Pure Flix made many films over the years and then transitioned into the streaming space, with its founders driving home the mission to inspire believers with biblical truth.

"Life is messy sometimes. We don't always know what's going to happen," Pure Flix co-founder Michael Scott once said. "If we invite God into those situations, He will clean up those messes ... You see God shows up in these situations."

Not every movie offers a Gospel presentation, though. And the level to which presentation evangelism is present in these faith and family-friendly movies can vary. But one thing is for certain: even the secular streaming services are employing Christians and faith-leaning content.

See, these companies see the financial value in tapping into audiences. Regardless, the creators — when they're authentic Christians with a mission to spread the Gospel — have a newfound ability to reach the masses with biblical truth.

While 2014 was initially dubbed the "year of the Bible" in entertainment due to "God's Not Dead" and a slew of other faith-related content, 10 years later, the entertainment space is gearing up for an even riper evangelistic opportunity.

"The Chosen," a TV series about Jesus and His followers, has inspired millions (and sparked some controversy along the way). But the show has made history on a number of fronts and has landed the Bible in places and spaces it's not traditionally seen.

"My heart is for people around the world to see an authentic portrayal of Jesus that draws them closer to the Bible and the real Jesus," "The Chosen" creator Jenkins has said.[91]

And that mission is being carried out through the Come and See Foundation, the organization responsible for spreading "The Chosen" across the globe. Stan Jantz, chief executive officer of the Come and See Foundation, told CBN News he wants to see the show reach 1 billion people.[92]

In addition to completing seven seasons of the show, Jantz said the team seeks to form global partnerships and "translate every episode of every season into 600 languages," something that hasn't ever been done on such a massive scale.[93]

"We're excited about ... Bible engagement," he said, explaining how the show is pushing people to read the Bible on YouVersion, a Scripture-engagement app. "YouVersion is finding a real uptick in their Bible engagement by showing 'The Chosen' on their apps."[94]

Again, regardless of where people stand on the show itself, it's impossible to deny it has been an effective piece of presentation evangelism.

And when it comes to tailored examples of this form of outreach, we must also consider some of the powerful ways the Gospel is strategically brought to specific groups of people.

"The Chosen" provides a wonderful example of how this works,

91   CBN News, "Dallas Jenkins Responds, Wants 'The Chosen' to Draw People 'Closer to the Bible and the Real Jesus,'" CBN News, accessed February 9, 2025, https://cbn.com/news/entertainment/dallas-jenkins-responds-wants-chosen-draw-people-closer-bible-and-real-jesus.
92   Billy Hallowell, "'The Chosen' Makes Big Announcement Amid Streaming Delay, Quest to Bring Show to One Billion People," Faithwire, March 14, 2024, accessed February 9, 2025, https://www.faithwire.com/2024/03/14/the-chosen-makes-big-announcement-amid-streaming-delay-quest-to-bring-show-to-one-billion-people/.
93   Hallowell, "'The Chosen' Makes Big Announcement."
94   Hallowell, "'The Chosen' Makes Big Announcement."

with Prison Fellowship — an organization ministering to inmates and their families — partnering to bring the show into prisons across the U.S.

Prison Fellowship itself is unique in its efforts to engage in presentation evangelism with prisoners, tailoring programs to their needs. The organization does simple outreach through prison chaplains and also hosts more complex evangelistic efforts.

The creation of Floodlight is perhaps one of the more intriguing developments, as the streaming platform – created during the COVID-19 pandemic — brings sermons and TV shows like "The Chosen" to inmates.

Then there's the Angel Tree outreach, a Christian endeavor that empowers churches to "strengthen relationships between incarcerated parents and their children and support the families of prisoners year-round."

Prison Fellowship uses Angel Tree to encourage Christians to offer Christmas gifts to kids on behalf of their incarcerated parents, host sports camps, send kids to summer camp, and engage in other efforts — all aimed at showing the love of Christ to these kids and families.

Perhaps the most interesting piece of Prison Fellowship's history surrounds its founder, Charles Colson; he was an aide to President Richard Nixon "who served a seven-month sentence for a Watergate-related crime," according to the organization's website.[95]

According to a retelling of the motivation behind Prison Fellowship, Colson was one day writing a letter while imprisoned at Maxwell Federal Prison Camp.[96]

He was deep in thought when another prisoner named Archie yelled out his name and posed a question: "What are you going to do for guys like us when you get out?"[97]

Colson replied that he would help out and wouldn't forget, but

---

95 Prison Fellowship, "Overview and Factsheets," Prison Fellowship, accessed February 9, 2025, https://www.prisonfellowship.org/resources/media-information/overview-and-factsheets/.
96 Alyson R. Quinn, "Watergate: The Glorious Defeat of Chuck Colson," Prison Fellowship, April 16, 2020, accessed February 9, 2025, https://www.prisonfellowship.org/story/watergate-the-glorious-defeat-of-chuck-colson/.
97 Quinn, "Watergate: The Glorious Defeat of Chuck Colson."

Archie was skeptical and said "big shots" like Colson never remember people like him.

But Archie was wrong. Colson not only remembered, but two years later in 1976, he founded Prison Fellowship for the very purpose of helping bring inmates to Christ.

What Archie potentially didn't know in those moments was that a friend had given Colson a copy of Lewis' "Mere Christianity" after Watergate and before his arrest. Colson read the book and was captivated — so enthralled that he embraced Jesus.

"I spent an hour calling out to God," Colson said, reflecting on the weep-filled moments that led to his spiritual surrender. "I did not even know the right words. I simply knew that I wanted Him."[98]

Colson eventually pleaded guilty to obstruction of justice in a case surrounding Daniel Ellsberg — and served time over the ordeal. But just when he thought all was lost, God stepped in and used his story for one of the greatest evangelistic endeavors to ever unfold in prisons.

The former political operative later proclaimed, "God used my greatest defeat for His glory!"[99]

Because of his eventual reliance on the Lord, God used Colson's failure for His victory, turning it into one of the most stunning presentation evangelism efforts of the century.

One other fact must not be glossed over as we discuss Prison Fellowship. The entire ordeal is a powerful example of one man's decision to step out in presentation evangelism (Lewis) having an impact on the life of another (Colson).

It's fascinating that "Mere Christianity" served as the spark to bring Colson to faith and, in turn, help him find the passion — and compassion — needed to launch his prison effort. The same principle applies in our own circles, no matter how big or small.

When we step out in faith and find ways to spread the Gospel, the fruits of that labor will often multiply in the lives of others.

Prison Fellowship is, of course, just one example of tailored efforts to reach specific populations through presentation evangelism. There are organizations targeting everything from domestic violence survivors

---

98 Quinn, "Watergate: The Glorious Defeat of Chuck Colson."
99 Quinn, "Watergate: The Glorious Defeat of Chuck Colson."

to those struggling with substance abuse — or even families grappling with childhood illness.

Not every issue is as heavy, though, with groups like the Fellowship of Christian Athletes turning attention to helping men and women in sports. Their mission is simple: to present the Gospel to coaches and athletes.

They use the presentation gospel and have developed an evangelistic strategy that has moved in big ways all over the world. They are able to get the Gospel into schools where other ministries cannot go.

I myself was saved in 1983 through the ministry of the Fellowship of Christian Athletes after I was recruited to play college football at Bowling Green State University — yet another example of how stepping out in presentation evangelism yields a fertile crop.

When I was young, my mother dragged me to church, but I hated it because I thought it was drier than a milk bucket under a bowl, especially as a young and rambunctious junior high kid.

But once I reached Bowling Green State University in 1982, God started putting people in my path who would prove to open the floodgates to the Gospel in my life. At that time, I met a man named Mark Miller who became our offensive coordinator, and the campus pastor named Bruce Montgomery.

Miller was an NFL quarterback and also a former Bowling Green legend. He quickly became a spiritual father to me on and off the field.

By sharing their testimonies, Miller and Montgomery started to transform my perspective. At the same time, people everywhere on campus unexpectedly began to tell me about Jesus, helping drive home the messages I was hearing. Eventually, it all came together.

I will never forget what happened one day as I was walking down the university hall and noticed something — a picture of an offensive lineman, muddy, covered with sweat, after a game, kneeling in a locker room in prayer. The caption on the picture read, "A man is never bigger than when he's on his knees."

There was something about that statement that permeated my mind and soul. The Holy Spirit shot through my heart that day and I went back to my dormitory room and collapsed to my knees beside my bed, weeping and crying out to Jesus.

I said, "God, I don't know what you want to do with my life, but whatever you want me to do, I'll do it." I was baptized not long after, not knowing what the Lord had in store.

Suddenly, I was playing football — and living life — as a Christian, and it was all because of targeted presentation evangelism and the kindness of Miller and Montgomery who shared their lives and faith with me.

I finished my playing career and signed with an agent. I was getting some pro looks from the Browns and the Steelers, but I had lost my passion for playing football; all I wanted to do was tell people about Jesus.

The phone never rang but my call from the Lord certainly did. I soon went to Kentucky Christian University, studied for ministry — and embarked on the journey the Lord had for my life.

Here I am now, decades later, writing a book about how to evangelize, a true testament to the power that can come from fruitfully sharing the Gospel in compelling and targeted ways.

WORSHIP EVANGELISM

There is one final form of presentation evangelism I'd like to cover and it involves worship – the playing of music and singing for purposes of praising the Lord. Worship is another King's Gambit.

On Earth, it's called the sacrifice of praise. When we exalt the name of the Lord Jesus and thank Him for His goodness, it is something we will never do in heaven. In this life, we have pain and sorrow. When we lift up the name of Jesus, that sacrifice of flesh lights the fire on the altar of revival! When David fasted and prayed for the baby not to die and then it died, he still got up and worshiped the Lord. They thought he was crazy, but he understood the sacrifice of praise. It was the King's Gambit.

When we study revival history we will find that almost every revival move of God or outpouring of the Holy Spirit has included worship. The Cane Ridge revival, the Azusa Street revival, and, most recently, Asbury have been examples, along with many others.

At its core, worship evangelism is making music to glorify God, letting the Holy Spirit evangelize people in the process. The Lord's presence lives in the praise. Just ponder the emotions you feel while exposed to praise and worship music.

Sometimes, the lyrics, cadence of the music, and flow strike deep in our hearts, with the Lord speaking to us through not only the message — but also the music. There's a reason why so many churches include music in Sunday services; it's a powerful way to honor God.

His presence always comes when we lift up His name. We see an example of this concerning the story of King Jehosophat in 2 Chronicles 20.

Jehosophat, a king of Judah who followed God at the start of his reign, ended up forging a partnership with Ahab, the evil king of Israel. It doesn't end well when God's warnings aren't heeded and Jehoshaphat gets rebuked.

But then something interesting happens when a group of nations plans to go up against Judah. After Jehoshaphat seeks the Lord, he's told Judah will be victorious.[100]

"Ye shall not need to fight in this battle: set yourselves, stand ye still, and see the salvation of the Lord with you, O Judah and Jerusalem: fear not, nor be dismayed; to morrow go out against them: for the Lord will be with you," Jahaziel, whom he consults with, proclaims in 2 Chronicles 20:17 (KVJ).

Jehoshaphat trusted the Lord in this matter and consulted singers (i.e. worshippers), telling them to "praise the beauty of holiness as they went out before the army." He very literally told them to "praise the Lord" (verse 21).

And the results of engaging in worship were profound, with these singers and worship leaders essentially toppling Judah's enemies.

"When they began to sing and to praise, the Lord set ambushments against the children of Ammon, Moab, and mount Seir, which were come against Judah; and they were smitten," verse 22 reads, with verse 23 continuing, "For the children of Ammon and Moab stood up against the inhabitants of mount Seir, utterly to slay and destroy them: and when they had made an end of the inhabitants of Seir, every one helped to destroy another."

---

100 GotQuestions.org, "Who Was King Jehoshaphat in the Bible?" GotQuestions. org, accessed February 9, 2025, https://www.gotquestions.org/King-Jehoshaphat. html.

Thus, Judah's enemies destroyed one another, with worship music leading the way.

It's a powerful story ultimately about trust in the Lord, yet the musical element is fascinating, particularly as we consider worship evangelism.

Many people have learned the secret of evangelistic worship. Much like the battle we saw God fighting for Jehoshaphat and his people, many Christians today take worship bands into dark areas of cities and towns, deploying them to perform.

Then, they watch people come to Christ when they get touched by the presence of God — a presence that comes amid the power of the music.

This is now common with worship bands that fill stadiums such as Jesus Culture, Bethel Worship, Brandon Lake, Phil Wickham, Chris Tomlin, Kari Jobe, Jesus Image, among so many others.

The lyrics instill important messages that the music drives home in the hearts of believers and nonbelievers, alike. It's one of the most overlooked evangelistic tools.

With our discussion of presentation evangelism now coming to a close, we move to another form of Gospel-sparing: power evangelism.

POWER EVANGELISM

T HE CENTRAL GOAL of all evangelism is pretty simple: to share the Gospel the way that Jesus did.

Christ is the prototype of how God wants us to live in every way, including when it comes to addressing non-believers and sharing with them the Hope they need to embrace for eternal life.

Jesus did not simply tell people the Good News; He also demonstrated the love of God through miracles, signs, and wonders. He put action to His transformational words, exhibiting His power and taking actionable steps to show people what it truly meant.

The definition of miracles is easily understood as something God does that happens instantaneously and is beyond human explanation. Merriam-Webster more succinctly defines a miracle as "an extraordinary event manifesting divine intervention in human affairs."[101]

Jesus' miracles bred faith in those who witnessed them, and the power in Christ's name continues to hold the ability to provide healing 2,000 years later.

As for signs, we already spoke about Jesus showing His power through acts like turning water into wine — a miraculous move unveiling His power and a blatant proof He was the Messiah.

Signs and wonders are often used synonymously in their

---

101 Merriam-Webster. "Miracle." Merriam-Webster.com Dictionary. Accessed February 9, 2025. https://www.merriam-webster.com/dictionary/miracle.

application of works of God for people to believe He is love. Love isn't something God does; it's who He is! And, if you're looking for examples of wonders, look no further than Jesus walking on water, feeding thousands, or doing any of the other stunning works inexplicable by human standards.

These powerful moves are part of God's very character, with the Lord illustrating them throughout the Old Testament as well, with the parting of the Red Sea for the Hebrews' safe passage after their exit from Egypt serving as perhaps one of the most famous examples.

When it comes to miracles, signs, and wonders, Jesus never held back and, in the process, sparked belief and awe in the hearts and minds of those who observed His compassionate acts of power evangelism.

The juxtaposition between Christ's actions and the thoughts and perspectives of the religious leaders of the day is quite stunning.

As we see in Scripture, the Pharisees relied on spouting rules without power, but this wasn't Christ's way. Jesus healed the sick, raised the dead, and cast out demons. It's the ultimate example of putting actions to words, as Christ performed these miracles after clearly and consistently delivering the truth.

Hearing is one thing, but seeing the power of Jesus' wondrous works enabled many to believe the message. This is what power evangelism is all about, with its sway and persuasive appeal still at work in our world today.

We see one of the most compelling examples of power evangelism in John 20:29 (KJV) when (doubting) Thomas encounters the risen Christ.

The disciples, who had already seen Jesus after His resurrection, told Thomas what they observed, but he was skeptical that Jesus was appearing among them. He essentially said, "Unless I see in his hands the nail marks and put my fingers into them as well as the injury on his side, I'm not buying it" (verse 25).

Not long after this statement, Jesus appeared to Thomas and the disciples. In those moments, one imagines Thomas was quite stunned as Christ met him where he was and implored him to, "Reach hither thy finger, and behold my hands; and reach hither thy hand, and thrust it into my side: and be not faithless, but believing" (verse 27).

Seeing, in this case, was believing, with Thomas responding by calling Jesus his "Lord" and "God." It was the ultimate moment of power evangelism at work, with the fulfillment of Jesus' sacrifice being fully shown.

As we consider this faith-building interaction in the Gospel narrative, there's something that must not be lost on us. Christ says something quite telling in this portion of Scripture, affirming that many will be blessed when they believe without seeing.

"Thomas, because you have seen me, you've believed," Jesus said in verse 29. "Blessed are they that have not seen, and yet have believed."

This is true and yet it also sparks some important questions and caveats. Some assume all that's left in our world today is to simply believe and not see, contending the miracles and healings we see in Scripture have somehow ceased.

Yet there's definitive evidence these incredible actions continue to unfold all over the world today, offering hope and pointing people back to the power of the Gospel.

Make no mistake: the Holy Spirit is still actively and supernaturally at work in evangelistic efforts, leading to signs, wonders, and demonstrations of God's power. And these manifestations of holy power serve as a means to draw people to the faith.

1 Corthinians 4:20 (KJV) proclaims, "For the kingdom of God is not in word, but in power," exhibiting the actionable ways the Lord works to draw people closer to Him.

As part of understanding this power evangelism process, we must also explore how Scripture seems to indicate these works will continue *through believers.*

"Verily, verily, I say unto you, He that believeth on me, the works that I do shall he do also; and greater works than these shall he do; because I go unto my Father," John 14:12 (KJV) reads.

As we've covered, one of the most faith-building, evangelistic acts Jesus performed in the Bible was healing the sick — a measure He seemed to engage in everywhere He preached.

Matthew 8 is filled with stories about this form of Jesus' power evangelism, with the Savior of the world offering people both physical and spiritual healing.

The Scriptures within this chapter explain how Jesus healed all the sick and, in turn, fulfilled what was written by the Prophet Isaiah.

"When evening came, many who were demon-possessed were brought to him, and he drove out the spirits with a word and healed all the sick," Matthew 8:16 (NIV) reads, with verse 17 continuing: "This was to fulfill what was spoken through the prophet Isaiah: 'He took up our infirmities and bore our diseases.'"[102]

This is referencing a fulfillment of Old Testament prophecy, with the latter Scripture pointing back to Isaiah 53:4 (KJV) which reads, "Surely he hath borne our griefs, and carried our sorrows: yet we did esteem him stricken, smitten of God, and afflicted."

Jesus secured our eternity; His powerful acts were also seen in His earthly ministry and by the Holy Spirit in, through, and around believers today.

God is still healing physical and spiritual illnesses, drawing others to Him in the process, regardless of what some might argue to the contrary.

In fact, every evangelist must know it is God's will to heal the sick just like it's His will for all to be saved. There is not one example in the Scriptures of someone who was brought to Jesus whom He intentionally didn't heal or to whom He showed disinterest in helping.

As Christians, we can simply command whatever infirmity or sickness to be healed — in the name of Jesus. Christ's name is our spiritual "police badge," coming along with faith-building and life-sustaining power.

To avoid disappointment, we must understand the difference between a miracle and a healing. A healing takes place over time. Sometimes, in the battle for healing and faith on Earth, our healings are completed in heaven. Just like everyone doesn't get instantly saved, not everyone is instantly healed.

We must keep the faith and always keep praying for the kingdom to come on earth as it is in heaven. Remember what Paul said in Galatians 3:5: Did God work miracles among you because you obeyed the law? The answer is obviously not! God does miracles because we believe

---

102   The Holy Bible, New International Version (Grand Rapids: Zondervan, 2011), Matthew 8.

what we've heard about him. He loves us. Satan attacks us with sickness and infirmity to destroy our faith in a good God.

JESUS' MANY HEALING ACTS

Circling back: some of the most intriguing facets of Matthew 8 are the different types and forms of healing Jesus performed. At the start of the chapter, readers encounter a leper who approaches Jesus and asks to be cleansed.

We're told Christ touched him and "immediately his leprosy was cleansed."

Then, we meet a centurion whose servant is sick. Christ offered to go to heal the servant, but the centurion — in a stunning show of faith — asked Jesus to merely speak the healing, believing wholeheartedly his servant would be made well.

Christ immediately "marveled" at this level of belief and said He had "not found so great faith" in Israel. Christ, of course, healed the servant that very hour.

And the healings didn't stop there. Peter's mother-in-law, we learn, was also sick with a fever. At this point, I'm sure you either know the story or could guess what happened next: Jesus touched her hand and she was healed. She even got up and started serving Him!

Next up, Jesus shifted to the spiritual, with people bringing those "possessed with devils" to Him, and He promptly cast demons out "with His word" (while, of course, continuing to heal the sick). We get a more specific demonic interaction in Matthew 8:28 when Jesus meets two individuals possessed by demons.

The two, who come to meet Jesus, are described as "coming out of the tombs, exceeding fierce, so that no man might pass by that way." These demons recognized Jesus' power as well, calling him "Son of God" and questioning whether He had come to torment them.

The demonic entities asked Christ to send them from the men into a herd of pigs — a request He granted.

There's much that could be written on that interaction, but here's the point: This is just one of the many stories we see in Scripture showing Jesus healing people from the throes of evil — and it's a compelling example of power evangelism. And such manifestations continue.

Centuries after that healing, Christians today will very likely encounter such demonic control of people while preaching the Gospel.

Demons have the ability to get control of people's minds, speaking lies into the hearts of their targets — diabolical mistruths people will tragically start to believe. These vile sentiments can impact people at various levels ranging from minor oppression to total control. We see the latter in the aforementioned example of Jesus healing the men.

When a person is not born again and Spirit-led, his or her heart and mind are not aligned with Christ and can more easily come under demonic control.

Therefore, we see such absurd behavior in the lives of people today. It is not simply that they are making bad decisions; these individuals are many times being controlled and influenced to do abnormal, problematic, and immoral things.

And every evangelist and Christian today must absolutely know and discern this dynamic.

In an era when too many churches avoid discussing the impact of evil, these realities are essential to understanding spiritual dynamics and how power evangelism can heal. There's much debate and discussion around the parameters of evil in the modern era, but we can look to Jesus' own work during His earthly ministry to discern and understand how it works in our world today.

Expelling the demonic was common throughout Jesus' ministry, with Scripture even showing ties between physical and spiritual illness. An example is seen in Luke 13:10-17 when we meet a woman who had a spirit of infirmity that made her cripple for 18 years.

Jesus, as He compassionately did throughout Scripture, rebuked the demon of infirmity, — and she was healed.

"And when Jesus saw her, he called her to him, and said unto her, Woman, thou art loosed from thine infirmity," Luke 13:12 (KJV) reads. "And he laid his hands on her: and immediately she was made straight, and glorified God."

There are countless additional examples, with Paul also expelling demons in Jesus' name. In fact, we see Paul discussing what it means to knock down strongholds in 2 Corinthians 10:3-5 (KJV), which reads:

| For though we walk in the flesh, we do not war after the flesh:

> (For the weapons of our warfare are not carnal, but mighty through God to the pulling down of strong holds;) Casting down imaginations, and every high thing that exalteth itself against the knowledge of God, and bringing into captivity every thought to the obedience of Christ.

This discussion is further expounded upon in Ephesians 6, a Bible chapter every Christian must fully comprehend, as it explains the spiritual nature of much of the chaos and consternation happening around us.

"Put on the whole armour of God, that you may be able to stand against the wiles of the devil," Ephesians 6:11 (KJV) reads. Verse 12 continues, "For we wrestle not against flesh and blood, but against principalities, against powers, against the rulers of the darkness of this world, against spiritual wickedness in high places."

Paul implores believers to put on the "whole armor of God" so we will be ready and equipped to withstand evil and cling to truth. The chapter makes a few realities clear:

1. There's a spiritual realm that impacts the physical life around us.
2. We must rely on a relationship with Christ for protection.
3. The devil will throw "darts" and attempt to thwart us.
4. The shield of faith (Christ) is available to us all.

Understanding these dynamics helps us focus on the reality beyond what our eyes can see and also helps further bring credence to the sway of power evangelism in the modern era.

In addition to boundless examples of power evangelism in the modern era, faith pioneers like Smith Wigglesworth, a Pentecostal revivalist from the United Kingdom who lived from 1859 until he died in 1947, provide rich examples of what it looks like to exemplify faith through Christ's power.

"Thousands came to Christian faith in his meetings, hundreds were healed of serious illnesses and diseases as supernatural signs followed his ministry," a biography reads. "A deep intimacy with his heavenly

Father and an unquestioning faith in God's Word brought spectacular results and provided an example for all true believers of the Gospel."[103]

There are many stories about Wigglesworth's healings and miracles, though Charisma covered one such story from Stanley H. Frodsham's "Smith Wigglesworth: Apostle of Faith," pondering whether it might be the "most incredible" of miracles attributed to him.

In a personal account, Wigglesworth recalled a man named Mr. Clark whom he described as a "very devoted brother." Clark was saddened and came to Wigglesworth one day to reveal his wife was dying and that he was struggling to believe in God for her healing.

Wigglesworth, though, wasn't dissuaded. He started to look for someone else to go with him to pray over Clark's wife, intent on trying to seek her healing. First, a fellow Christian named Howe declined to go with Wigglesworth, but told him, "I believe if you will go, God will heal."

Seeing this as an encouragement, Wigglesworth then approached a man named Nichols who agreed to go with him to Clark's wife. By the time they reached her home, she was "nearly gone." And here's the interesting thing: Clark and Nichols reportedly didn't believe in divine healing — but that didn't stop Wigglesworth.[104]

"Though I knew that neither Clark nor Nichols believed in Divine Healing, I had concealed a small bottle in my hip pocket that would hold about half a pint of oil," he said in his account. "I put a long cork in it so that I could open the bottle easily. I took the bottle out of my pocket and held it behind me, and said: 'Now you pray, Mr. Clark.' Brother Clark, being encouraged by Brother Nichols' prayer, prayed also that he might be sustained in his great bereavement."[105]

Wigglesworth had to repeatedly stop the prayers, as they had to shift their focus to help Clark and his children once the wife was gone — and not on healing.

"As soon as he stopped, I pulled the cork out of the bottle, and went over to the dying woman who was laid out on the bed," he said.

---

103 Smith Wigglesworth, "Smith Wigglesworth: The Apostle of Faith," accessed February 9, 2025, https://smithwigglesworth.com/.
104 Stanley Howard Frodsham, Smith Wigglesworth: Apostle of Faith (Springfield, MO: Gospel Publishing House, 1948).
105 Frodsham, Smith Wigglesworth: Apostle of Faith.

"I was a novice at this time and did not know any better, so I poured all the contents of that bottle of oil over Mrs. Clark's body in the name of Jesus!"

Now, here's where the account takes a stunning turn. Wigglesworth claims Jesus appeared near the foot of the wife's bed.

"I had my eyes open gazing at Him," he said. "There He was at the foot of the bed. He gave me one of those gentle smiles. I see Him just now as I tell this story to you. I have never lost that vision, the vision of that beautiful soft smile."[106]

If that weren't incredible enough, the healing Clark and Nichols presumably thought was impossible came to fruition, with Wigglesworth claiming the wife was "raised up and filled with life, and lived to bring up a number of children." He said she also "outlived her husband many years," offering quite a stunning reminder of what power evangelism can look like.

Healings, whether physical or spiritual, are a key part of signs and wonders and obviously fall under the category of miracles.

---

106 Frodsham, Smith Wigglesworth: Apostle of Faith.

174

PROPHETIC EVANGELISM

"PROPHETIC EVANGELISM IS *simply God using revelatory phenomena to speak to the hearts of those who don't know Jesus."*

That's how Mark Stibbe described prophetic evangelism, explaining how believers were given newfound power to witness about Jesus when God granted the Holy Spirit on the Day of Pentecost.[107]

When we talk about prophecy, we're speaking about messages given and infused by the Lord. As Stibbe added, "Prophecy is the ability to receive and declare revelation from God."[108]

When discussing prophetic evangelism, I often look to Ezekiel 37 and the Valley of Dry Bones. It's in that chapter we see God bring Ezekiel out in the spirit and set him in the middle of a valley of dry, dead, and very old bones.

One can picture a graveyard of sorts while reading these verses, with the bones of humans lying in piles upon one another — a mass symbol of disconnectedness and death that unfolded long ago.

Interestingly, God asks Ezekiel something after showing him this scene: "Can these bones live?" Of course, no mere mortal could make bones — the leftovers long after human decomposition has concluded

---

107 "Prophetic Evangelism," Premier Christianity, accessed February 9, 2025, https://www.premierchristianity.com/home/prophetic-evangelism/1560.article.
108 "Prophetic Evangelism."

— live again. Only the resurrection power of the Holy Spirit could give such life to the dead, which we see play out in the subsequent verses.

Ezekiel 37:5-8 (KJV) explains what happened next:

> Thus saith the Lord God unto these bones; Behold, I will cause breath to enter into you, and ye shall live: And I will lay sinews upon you, and will bring up flesh upon you, and cover you with skin, and put breath in you, and ye shall live; and ye shall know that I am the Lord.

> So I prophesied as I was commanded: and as I prophesied, there was a noise, and behold a shaking, and the bones came together, bone to his bone. And when I beheld, lo, the sinews and the flesh came up upon them, and the skin covered them above: but there was no breath in them.

Now, we see the image of fully-formed human bodies; what seemed impossible is now reality, with the Lord drawing it all together. Next, God tells Ezekiel to prophesy to these bones and say to them, "Dry bones, hear the word of the Lord."

God said He would make breath enter the bones and they would come to life. Ezekiel listened to the Lord's prompting, proclaiming in verse 10 (KJV): "So, I prophesied as he commanded me, and the breath came into them, and they lived, and stood up upon their feet, an exceeding great army."

The imagery these verses spark is quite stunning, as readers are left imagining these bones reconnecting and reforming, with flesh covering them and the breath of life suddenly emerging in the resurrected's lungs.

Some readers might ponder what in the world could be going on here — what the deeper meaning might be. As the verses progress, we see this when God then tells Ezekiel the bones are representative of the "whole house of Israel," noting that the people believed their bones were "dried," their hope was "lost" and they were "cut off."

One must consider the state of Israel then to fully comprehend what's unfolding here. With the nation tattered, divided, and in chaos during the Babylonian captivity, GotQuestions perhaps best captures the situation: "[Israel] had been divided and dispersed for so long that unification and restoration seemed impossible."[109]

But amid that pain, God gave Ezekiel a prophetic message to deliver — one that has captivated Jews and Christians for thousands of years now.

"Therefore prophesy and say unto them, Thus saith the Lord God; Behold, O my people, I will open your graves, and cause you to come up out of your graves, and bring you into the land of Israel," verse 12 reads (KJV), with verses 13-14 continuing: "And ye shall know that I am the Lord, when I have opened your graves, O my people, and brought you up out of your graves. And shall put my spirit in you, and ye shall live, and I shall place you in your own land: then shall ye know that I the Lord have spoken it, and performed it, saith the Lord."

These prophetic messages go on to speak about a gathering of the "children of Israel from among the heathen" and the regathering of them all — as one nation — back in Israel.

The Lord was essentially telling Ezekiel the whole house of Israel would be "born again," with that emerging in the physical (literal placement of Jews back in Israel in 1948) and the spiritual (the coming of Jesus which brought Christianity to fruition and created a path for Jews and Gentiles, alike).

Ezekiel's interaction with the Lord is a prime example of prophetic evangelism.

Under this form of evangelism, we call those who are dead in their sins and prophesy to them by the word of the Lord.

Prophetic evangelism is learning to see the lost — people who are nothing but dry bones — become fully-fleshed Christians, with spiritual tendons, skin, and breath. These folks, when they accept Christ, become born again and members of the Lord's army. It's a form of evangelism I've seen throughout my ministry, and also in my everyday interactions in life.

A few years ago, while subbing at a high school, my assignment was to teach government. If I'm being honest, the entire day was filled with high school juniors who were quite bored with the class.

---

109 GotQuestions.org, "What Is the Meaning of the Valley of Dry Bones in Ezekiel 37?" GotQuestions.org, accessed February 9, 2025, https://www.gotquestions.org/valley-dry-bones.html.

I found myself in an intriguing position. There, in that classroom, class after class was lethargically coming through to talk about a subject in which they had little interest. As I was teaching one day, something interesting happened.

In two of the specific classes, I felt compelled to tell the teens that they are the most global generation to ever hit the planet. And that, out of their brokenness — a disconnectedness no one can deny exists within our young people today — they would find their identity and become some of the greatest leaders the planet has ever seen.

I told them God had made them special to be one nation under Him and indivisible just like the pledge we say every morning. They would create new and great inventions that would save people; they would foster a new culture of love without fear that helps and serves all. And that this love would never fail. I told them not even death could take away their right to believe in God.

I gave two sermons that day without ever mentioning the name of Jesus. But under the prompting of the Holy Spirit, I proclaimed with great compassion and love for them how great they would be in the future. The Bible calls moments like this "prophesying" — calling the things that are not as if they were.

It's something that must happen under the guidance of the Holy Spirit and with the Lord's revelation. These aren't flippant comments that come from our own hearts; instead, they are messages from the Lord we are to deliver to those around us — and the impact can be profound.

Take, for instance, my own experience in the classroom that day. I was simply not prepared for what would happen to those high school juniors. The Holy Spirit fell in the classrooms and the presence of Jesus was thick.

I wish I had the entirety of the experience on film. I have done TV and radio broadcasts and am well aware of the awkwardness and danger of "dead" air time — when there is a silent pause and no one says anything for what seems like an eternity.

We had a silence in the rooms after I spoke that day — but it exposed how deep these messages permeated.

I will never forget literally timing how long the students went silent after I spoke. For three minutes, students could not speak. I wondered what they were feeling deep inside as the eyes of many were watering.

I'll never forget watching the face and eyes of one teen in particular, a young Hispanic kid who always loved to help people. I called him the Cruiser. After three minutes of no one speaking I asked him: "Cruiser, what do you think this is?" And I will never forget his answer: "I don't know, man, but whatever this is, it is real."

"It is real." Those words deeply resonated. In a world and culture with so much fakery, deceit, and confusion being catapulted at these kids, those simple, prophetic words about their future gave them a deep, profound, and authentic hope only God can deliver.

See, when you speak with the prophetic spirit of the Lord Jesus who sees the best in people, you can prophesy the gold instead of the dirt. As disciples of Jesus, we are treasure hunters. When you're looking for gold you're going to remove a lot of dirt but we all must always remember we are not looking for the dirt; we're on the prowl for something far greater!

Speak to the dry bones the Word of the Lord and say, "Jesus is the resurrection and the life." Those students that day got a taste of this truth, and there are many others in your life desperate to be the recipients of prophetic evangelism; they're simply waiting for an "Ezekiel" to relay the message.

But Christians do not have to be prophets to call out the best in people. You just know that one of the baits in the tackle box is prophetically sharing the Gospel with those who are dead in their sins. The Holy Spirit equips you to help build up the army of God.

PROPHETIC EVANGELISM OVER BELIEVERS

This form of evangelism isn't just about prophesying over unbelievers, though, as Christians can also use it to spiritually serve one another.

Years ago, while at a youth conference in Michigan, I was with a friend of mine named Louie. He was a Bible college professor and a national speaker popular at many youth conferences. Louie was preaching that day and he had asked me to lead ministry time.

So, during that time, we invited kids to give their lives to Christ.

But something else happened that day unrelated to the kids at the conference. The Holy Spirit had highlighted to me a young married couple who were youth pastors at their church.

We called them forward and were shocked to find out they had been reading the Book of Acts and discovering the power of the Holy Spirit — only to encounter pushback within their home church.

See, the young couple had been accused by their church of being under the spirit of the antichrist because they began believing in the power of the Holy Spirit. That particular church did not share in such beliefs and, thus, a theological rift emerged.

We prayed for this couple, connected, and then also prayed alongside them. I don't even remember the words that were spoken over them, yet the story stands out in my heart and mind.

Not long after that encounter, I called the young man for whom we had prayed tando invited him to join us on staff at our church. I was the associate pastor and didn't even have the authority to do that, but I felt an unordinary push from the Lord to bring them in.

As God always does, He was prophetically moving the chess pieces around. Little did I know at the time, but my phone call to the couple came at the exact time they had submitted their resignation letter to the leaders at their church.

The rest became history! They joined us for two years and became fixtures in our work. That initial prompting at the youth conference paved a path we wouldn't have taken had we not engaged in prophetic evangelism.

After the couple worked at our church, Louie then chose the young man to take over a network he had started. That network has now grown beyond what we could've ever imagined and today is known as The Nfluence Network. This couple — Lucas and Krissy Miles — have become national Bible teachers, speakers, and authors.

Lucas is very gifted at encouraging pastors and leaders and evangelizing people who are deceived by the cult of Woke Christianity. It's inspiring to see how the Lord has used that initial prophetic moment to help usher Lucas and Krissy to where they are today.

That is how God works; He connects people and ties the knots of the intersecting ropes to create a fishnet that catches way more fish than a simple fishing pole ever could.

When we trust in the Lord's messages, He truly delivers.

Now the irony of God's fishnet is: decades later, I now work for Lucas and Krissy. Who would've ever guessed in one prophetic moment, kingdom evangelism would spark a relationship that would span decades, spark discipleship, and create powerful efforts to reach the lost with the Gospel.

One of the great keys of evangelism is the unity we find in Psalm 133 — a unity that sparks powerful spiritual opportunities. That chapter reads (KJV):

> Behold, how good and how pleasant it is for brethren to dwell together in unity!
>
> It is like the precious ointment upon the head, that ran down upon the beard, even Aaron's beard: that went down to the skirts of his garments;
>
> As the dew of Hermon, and as the dew that descended upon the mountains of Zion: for there the Lord commanded the blessing, even life for evermore.

If we want to make disciples out of nations and cities then we are going to have to unite as Christ's church and prophetically cast the King's fishnet for the miraculous harvest of souls.

The oil represented here in Psalm 133 is the anointing which is the ability of God to bring heaven to Earth and destroy the works of the devil. And prophesy bones will live! All we need to do is listen.

CONCLUSION:
THE END TIME MYSTERY OF
EVANGELISM

THE KING'S GAMBIT was Christ's sacrifice on the cross that defeated the devil forever.

Now, His Kingdom reigns forever over the last bit of rebellion on earth. The church — the disciples of Jesus — have been suffering at the hands of the devil since the Holy Spirit came to dwell in all believers.

The King is the bridegroom and His gambit is finished. The Queen is the church who has now suffered for centuries enduring persecutions, imprisonments, projections and even martyrdom. This has stored up a sevenfold justice that is placed upon the devil and his dark kingdom (Proverbs 6:31).

This is the Queen's gambit: To live is Christ and to die is gain. And it's really all just a checkmate. Sing the doxology — "Hallelujah!"

No matter what our end time theology, we have two solid stakes in the ground that we don't get to vote on. That is guaranteed in the word of God.

1. Jesus will return and destroy all evil.
2. It will happen sooner than we think and when we least expect it.

As we round out to a close, I must reflect upon a moment I call the "911 emergency scream" – a stunning event that had a profound impact on me.

In July 2017, while cleaning up a trash pile in my backyard, I heard an unmistakable, audible scream. Three times the supernatural voice screamed my name, "Vic! Vic! Vic!"

There was no one else outside other than my wife on the other end of our acre property, so I naturally thought it was her. I thought she had been hurt and that we would undoubtedly be headed for the emergency room.

My daughter Bekah heard the screams as well. So, she, too, sprinted to her mother's rescue. I jumped in my truck and drove to the other end of our property. When we reached my wife, Shelley, she was bewildered and looked completely mystified.

Not only was she completely healthy and fine, but she had heard nothing. The scream Bekah and I heard wasn't even on her radar. Oddly, there was no one else around for miles that afternoon, thus no human could have yelled my name that many times.

I immediately knew it was an angel, but I was confused as to what had unfolded. I remember sitting down in my chair around 2:30 p.m. that afternoon. I said, "God, what am I supposed to do with that? What did that mean? What do You want."

The answers didn't immediately come to me, but, the next day, a good friend of mine, George Williams, was filling the pulpit at my church. His sermon was a plea to the body of Christ to win souls before it's too late. The time is running out, he said.

As he delivered the message, I suddenly understood: God is screaming for His church to win souls for Christ! The return of the Lord Jesus will be soon. Much sooner than we expect! And that's a message that hasn't been lost on me.

It is my prayer that this book serves not only as an encouragement and blessing, but also as an evangelistic tool offering you the blueprint, tips, and guidance needed to enhance your relationship with the Lord while simultaneously reaching the lost.

From exploring the prevalence of evil in our world to exploring hints of revival and an unquenched thirst for Jesus — to evangelistic advice – it is my hope that "The King's Gambit" is an indispensable resource for believers everywhere.

As we come to a close, we must remember the three commissions I believe we have from Jesus. First and foremost, there's Christ's command in Matthew 28:18-20 — that we go into all the world to make disciples.

Second, we are called to heal the sick, raise the dead, cast out demons, preach the kingdom (Matthew 10:1). And, finally, I believe we're called to be baptized in the Holy Spirit to receive power to be His witnesses, with the power of all of the gifts infusing our faith walks (Acts 1:8).

"We have not because we ask not." That's a mantra we must comprehend as we look at what we're called to do and juxtapose it against how the church sometimes behaves today.

It's essential the American church realize why evangelism in our nation has too often so miserably failed. Our unbelief and refusal to heed the aforementioned calls has led to the rejection of two of the commissions of Jesus.

Many of us reject the notion we can heal the sick, raise the dead, cast out demons and have made theologies to justify our unbelief.

Plus, the rejection of baptism in the Holy Spirit to receive power to be His witnesses has rendered the American church spiritually ineffective or, at the least, tragically deficient.

Jesus' theology must become our own, and Christ's pattern, as observed in Scripture, is clear: He displayed the kingdom's power by healing diseases, casting out demons, and raising their dead. Plus, He broke down the Gospel message in compelling form.

In America, we must repent of our unbelief and return to the King's Gospel, reflecting these sentiments in our own evangelistic pursuits.

Our churches in America are filled with testimonies about what Jesus did, which is powerful. But the tragedy is too many of our churches have no testimonies of what Christians do through Christ.

We hear about Jesus' miracles in church, but what's missing is how God is working through believers today — just as He did the early church — to perform the miraculous.

After 40 years of pastoring and preaching, I can testify the awkwardness that sometimes emerges when I ask congregations, "Has anyone experienced a miraculous testimony they would like to share?"

Sadly, crickets rather than stories filled with the miraculous love of God tend to follow.

We must return to faith in the power of the name of Jesus above all names. The name of Jesus is the ultimate "police badge." All authority in heaven and earth has been given to Him, and He, in turn, has given it to us. God died to make men holy; let us live to make men free! Come quickly, Lord Jesus. Amen.

Works Cited

The Birth Pains

Billy Graham Library. "10 Quotes from Billy Graham on World Evangelism." *Billy Graham Library Blog*, August 17, 2023. https://billygrahamlibrary.org/blog-10-quotes-from-billy-graham-on-world-evangelism/.

Billy Graham Library, "10 Quotes from Billy Graham."

The Light of the Church

Gallup. "Moral Issues." Gallup News, 2024. https://news.gallup.com/poll/1681/moral-issues.aspx.

Gallup, "Moral Issues."

Gallup, "Moral Issues."

Gallup, "Moral Issues."

Barna Group. "Competing Worldviews Influence Today's Christians." Barna, May 9, 2017. https://www.barna.com/research/competing-worldviews-influence-todays-christians/.

Barna Group, "Competing Worldviews."

Barna Group, "Competing Worldviews."

Hallowell, Billy. "God, Truth, Sin, and Church: Shocking Study Reveals How Americans' Shifting Views Are Sparking Biblical

Worldview Crisis." Faithwire, May 18, 2023. https://www.
faithwire.com/2023/05/18/god-truth-sin-and-church-shocking-
study-reveals-how-americans-shifting-views-are-sparking-biblical-
worldview-crisis/.

Hallowell, "God, Truth, Sin, and Church."

Hallowell, Billy. "'Shocking' Shift Among Born-Again Christians
on Jesus' Sinless Nature: Pastors Would Be Wise to 'Rebuild the
Spiritual Foundation.'" Faithwire, April 24, 2023. https://www.
faithwire.com/2023/04/24/shocking-shift-among-born-again-
christians-on-jesus-sinless-nature-pastors-would-be-wise-to-re-
build-the-spiritual-foundation/.

Methodist Church in Britain. ILG Designed Update, December
2023. Archived January 17, 2024. Accessed February 9, 2025.
https://web.archive.org/web/20240117111250/https://www.
methodist.org.uk/media/31380/ilg-designed-update-de-
cember-2023.pdf.

Methodist Church in Britain, ILG Designed Update.

Winfield, Nicole. "Christian Denominations Are Divided on
Blessing Same-Sex Unions. Here's Where They Stand." Associated
Press News, December 24, 2023. https://apnews.com/article/
lgbtq-samesex-unions-christianity-catholic-anglican-method-
ist-00e3a4adaf4266dabbf730390eebd2d9.

Winfield, "Christian Denominations on Same-Sex Unions."

Winfield, "Christian Denominations on Same-Sex Unions."

Reverberations of Revival

Hallowell, Billy. "'There Is Revival': Evangelist Has 'Never
Seen Anything' Like Spiritual Reformation Sweeping
America." Faithwire, January 5, 2024. https://www.faithwire.
com/2024/01/05/thereis-revival-evangelist-has-never-seen-any-
thing-like-spiritual-reformation-sweeping-america/.

Pew Research Center. "How U.S. Religious Composition
Has Changed in Recent Decades." Pew Research

Center: Religion & Public Life, September 13, 2022. https://www.pewresearch.org/religion/2022/09/13/how-u-s-religious-composition-has-changed-in-recent-decades/.

Pew Research Center, "U.S. Religious Composition."

Asbury University. "Outpouring." Asbury University, 2023. https://www.asbury.edu/outpouring/.

Hallowell, Billy. "'Our Culture's Going to Be Changed': Massive Revival at Asbury University Captivates World, Shows No Signs of Slowing Down." Faithwire, February 14, 2023. https://www.faithwire.com/2023/02/14/our-cultures-going-to-be-changed-massive-revival-at-asbury-university-captivates-world-shows-no-signs-of-slowing-down/.

Asbury University, "Outpouring."

Hallowell, Billy. "'A Sweet Move of God': Actor and Filmmaker Alex Kendrick Sees Power of Revival Firsthand at Lee University, Praises Experience." Faithwire, February 27, 2023. https://www.faithwire.com/2023/02/27/a-sweet-move-of-god-actor-and-film-maker-alex-kendrick-sees-power-of-revival-firsthand-at-lee-univer-sity-praises-experience/.

Biola University. "What Is Christian Revival? Three Resources to Help You Understand Revival." Good Book Blog, March 2, 2023. https://www.biola.edu/blogs/good-book-blog/2023/what-is-chris-tian-revival-three-resources-to-help-you-understand-revival.

Biola University, "What Is Christian Revival?"

Foust, Michael. "Asbury Prof: 'Outpouring,' Not 'Revival,' Is Best Label for Recent Events." Crosswalk, February 28, 2023. https://www.crosswalk.com/headlines/contributors/michael-foust/asbury-prof-outpouring-not-revival-is-best-label-for-recent-events.html.

Encyclopaedia Britannica. "Second Great Awakening." Britannica, 2024. https://www.britannica.com/topic/Second-Great-Awakening.

Encyclopaedia Britannica. "Great Awakening." Britannica, 2024. https://www.britannica.com/event/Great-Awakening.

History.com Editors. "Great Awakening." History, A&E Television Networks, last modified October 10, 2019. https://www.history.com/topics/european-history/great-awakening.

Christianity.com Editors. "The Great Awakening." Christianity.com, Salem Web Network. Accessed February 9, 2025. https://www.christianity.com/church/church-history/timeline/1701-1800/the-great-awakening-11630212.html.

Bill of Rights Institute. "The Great Awakening." Bill of Rights Institute. Accessed February 9, 2025. https://billofrightsinstitute.org/essays/the-great-awakening.

Bill of Rights Institute, "The Great Awakening."

Hallowell, Billy. "85-Year-Old Man Whose Family Thought He'd Never Find Jesus Gets Baptized at Greg Laurie's Historic Event: 'Never Give Up on People.'" Faithwire, July 12, 2023. https://www.faithwire.com/2023/07/12/85-year-old-man-whose-family-thought-hed-never-find-jesus-gets-baptized-at-greg-lauries-historic-event-never-give-up-on-people/.

Hallowell, "85-Year-Old Man Gets Baptized."

Hallowell, Billy. "Can Another Great Awakening Unfold if End-Times Prophecy Says Things Will Worsen? Greg Laurie on Why a 'Jesus Revolution' Is Possible." Faithwire, March 3, 2023. https://www.faithwire.com/2023/03/03/can-another-great-awakening-unfold-if-end-times-prophecy-says-things-will-worsen-greg-laurie-on-why-a-jesus-revolution-is-possible/.

Hallowell, Billy. "Are the End Times Upon Us? Greg Laurie Breaks Down Why Understanding Bible Prophecy Is So Essential." Faithwire, March 8, 2022. https://www.faithwire.com/2022/03/08/are-the-end-times-upon-us-greg-laurie-breaks-down-why-understanding-bible-prophecy-is-so-essential/.

What Christians Get Wrong About Evangelism

Barna Group. "Sharing Faith Is Increasingly Optional for Christians." Barna, May 15, 2018. https://www.barna.com/research/sharing-faith-increasingly-optional-christians/.

Barna Group, "Sharing Faith Is Increasingly Optional."

Bible Gateway. "Mark 16:15, New International Version." Bible Gateway. Accessed February 9, 2025. https://www.biblegateway.com/passage/?search=Mark%2016%3A15&version=NIV.

Lifeway Research. Evangelism Explosion: Survey of American Christians Report. August 4, 2022. https://research.lifeway.com/wp-content/uploads/2022/08/Evangelism-Explosion-Survey-of-American-Christians-Report-8_4_22.pdf.

Kyriacou, Nicole Alcindor. "Two-Thirds of Christians Don't Know Methods for Sharing Jesus: Study." The Christian Post, August 9, 2022. https://www.christianpost.com/news/two-thirds-of-christians-dont-know-methods-for-sharing-jesus.html.

Barna Group. "Why Christians Don't Share Their Faith." Barna, Aug. 23, 2023. https://www.barna.com/research/christians-share-faith/.

Barna Group, "Why Christians Don't Share Their Faith."

Earls, Aaron. "Christians Don't Share Faith with Unchurched Friends." Lifeway Research, September 9, 2021. https://research.lifeway.com/2021/09/09/christians-dont-share-faith-with-unchurched-friends/.

Misunderstanding the Belong-Believe-Behave Model

GotQuestions.org. "What Is the Story of the Woman Caught in Adultery?" GotQuestions.org. Accessed February 9, 2025. https://www.gotquestions.org/woman-caught-in-adultery.html.

Stewart, Don. "Why Is the Story of the Woman Caught in Adultery Missing from Many Ancient Manuscripts?" Blue Letter Bible. Accessed February 9, 2025. https://www.blueletterbible.org/faq/don_stewart/don_stewart_1319.cfm.

GotQuestions.org. "Who Were the Samaritans?" GotQuestions. org. Accessed February 9, 2025. https://www.gotquestions.org/ Samaritans.html.

Gallup. "Moral Issues." Gallup News, 2024. Accessed February 9, 2025. https://news.gallup.com/poll/1681/moral-issues.aspx.

Our Failure to Remember: Salvation Doesn't Depend on Us
None

Our Failure to Rely on Prayer in Evangelism

The History of the Bible: How Did We Get the Bible?, YouTube video, 1:21:21, May 9, 2020, accessed February 9, 2025, https://www.youtube.com/watch?v=cgAadaFQtjk.

Life Action. "Five Things Billy Graham Did Not Do." Life Action, 2023. Accessed February 9, 2025. https://lifeaction.org/ five-things-billy-graham-did-not-do/.

Life Action, "Five Things Billy Graham Did Not Do."

Our Failure to Understand the Power of "Watering Holes" in Cities and Communities

Merriam-Webster. "Watering Hole." Merriam-Webster.com Dictionary. Accessed February 9, 2025. https://www.merri-am-webster.com/dictionary/watering%20hole.

National Center for Education Statistics. "Public School Enrollment." Condition of Education, May 2024. Accessed February 9, 2025. https://nces.ed.gov/programs/coe/indicator/cga/ public-school-enrollment.

Bible Gateway. "Proverbs 30, New International Version." Bible Gateway. Accessed February 9, 2025. https://www.biblegateway. com/passage/?search=Proverbs+30&version=NIV.

City of Wauseon. "LIGHT UP WAUSEON! Mayor Huner has requested that the Wauseon Star be put back up in South Park and lit. She is asking everyone to go outside..." Facebook, December 2018. Accessed February 9, 2025. https://www.

facebook.com/cityofwauseon/photos/a.226438851243263/62578
7804641697/.

Our Failure to Believe in Miracles, Signs, and Wonders
None

Our Failure to Realize There Are Many Different Baits in the Tackle Box
None

Apostolic Evangelism: Serving Like the Early Church
Hahn, Ferdinand. "On the Origin of the Term 'Apostolos.'" Novum
   Testamentum 3, no. 1 (1959): 293–300. https://www.jstor.org/
   stable/43714117.

Renner, Rick. "The Historical Meaning of the Word
   'Apostle'." Renner Ministries, October 25, 2024.
   Accessed February 9, 2025. https://renner.org/article/
   the-historical-meaning-of-the-word-apostle/.

Renner, "Historical Meaning of the Word 'Apostle'."

Bible Gateway. "Acts 25, English Standard Version." Bible Gateway.
   Accessed February 9, 2025. https://www.biblegateway.com/
   passage/?search=Acts+25%3A8&version=ESV.

Bible Gateway, "Acts 25, ESV."

Bible Gateway, "Acts 26, English Standard Version," Bible Gateway,
   accessed February 9, 2025, https://www.biblegateway.com/
   passage/?search=Acts+25%3A8&version=ESV.

Bible Gateway, "Acts 26, ESV."

Encyclopedia Britannica. "How Did St. Paul the Apostle Die?"
   Encyclopædia Britannica, accessed February 9, 2025. https://
   www.britannica.com/question/How-did-St-Paul-the-Apostle-die.

Understanding Prayer Evangelism

GotQuestions.org. "What Is the Lord's Prayer and Should We Pray It?" GotQuestions.org. Accessed February 9, 2025. https://www.gotquestions.org/Lords-prayer.html.

GotQuestions.org. "What Was the Babylonian Captivity/Exile?" GotQuestions.org. Accessed February 9, 2025. https://www.gotquestions.org/Babylonian-captivity-exile.html.

GotQuestions.org, "Babylonian Captivity/Exile."

Bible Gateway. "Acts 4:19–20, New International Version." Bible Gateway. Accessed February 9, 2025. https://www.biblegateway.com/passage/?search=Acts+4%3A19-20&version=NIV.

Presence Evangelism

Bible Gateway. "Romans 12:20, New International Version." Bible Gateway. Accessed February 9, 2025. https://www.biblegateway.com/passage/?search=Romans+12%3A20&version=NIV.

Bible Gateway. "Matthew 5:44, New International Version." Bible Gateway. Accessed February 9, 2025. https://www.biblegateway.com/passage/?search=Matthew+5%3A44&version=NIV.

Mother Teresa. "If you can't feed a hundred people, then feed just one." Goodreads. Accessed February 9, 2025. https://www.goodreads.com/quotes/9181130-if-you-can-t-feed-a-hundred-people-then-feed-just.

Operation Blessing. "What We Do." Operation Blessing. Accessed February 9, 2025. https://www.ob.org/what-we-do/.

Bernock, Danielle. "Why Did Jesus Turn Water into Wine?" Christianity.com, October 12, 2023. Accessed February 9, 2025. https://www.christianity.com/wiki/jesus-christ/why-did-jesus-turn-water-into-wine.html.

GotQuestions.org. "Why Did Jesus Choose the Wedding at Cana for His First Miracle?" GotQuestions.org. Accessed February 9, 2025. https://www.gotquestions.org/wedding-at-Cana.html.

Presentation Evangelism

Encyclopedia Britannica. "Kerygma and Catechesis." Encyclopædia Britannica. Accessed February 9, 2025. https://www.britannica.com/topic/kerygma.

Cru. "Cru Historical Fact Sheet." Cru. Accessed February 9, 2025. https://www.cru.org/us/en/about/cru-press/background/cru-historical-fact-sheet.html.

Cru, "Cru Historical Fact Sheet."

Cru. "Would You Like to Know God Personally?" Cru. Accessed February 9, 2025. https://www.cru.org/ph/en/how-to-know-god/would-you-like-to-know-god-personally1.html.

Cru, "Would You Like to Know God Personally?"

Billy Graham Library. "10 Quotes from Billy Graham on World Evangelism." Billy Graham Library, April 10, 2022. Accessed February 9, 2025. https://billygrahamlibrary.org/blog-10-quotes-from-billy-graham-on-world-evangelism/.

ABC News. "Rev. Billy Graham Counseled President Truman." ABC News, May 12, 2011. Accessed February 9, 2025. https://abcnews.go.com/Politics/rev-billy-graham-counseled-president-truman/story?id=13583583.

GotQuestions.org. "What Is Christian Apologetics?" GotQuestions.org. Accessed February 9, 2025. https://www.gotquestions.org/Christian-apologetics.html.

Josh.org. "Media Information." Josh.org. Accessed February 9, 2025. https://www.josh.org/about/media-information/.

Hallowell, Billy. "'Is God Real?': Famed Author Lee Strobel Explores Proof of God and the Bible." Faithwire, November 14, 2023. Accessed February 9, 2025. https://www.faithwire.com/2023/11/14/is-god-real-famed-author-lee-strobel-explores-proof-of-god-and-the-bible/.

Hallowell, "'Is God Real?'"

Lewis, C.S. Mere Christianity. New York: HarperOne, 2001.

Marsden, George. "A Biography of Mere Christianity." C.S. Lewis Institute, March 7, 2017. Accessed February 9, 2025. https://www.cslewisinstitute.org/resources/a-biography-of-mere-christianity/.

CBN News. "Dallas Jenkins Responds, Wants 'The Chosen' to Draw People 'Closer to the Bible and the Real Jesus.'" CBN News, accessed February 9, 2025. https://cbn.com/news/entertainment/dallas-jenkins-responds-wants-chosen-draw-people-closer-bible-and-real-jesus.

Hallowell, Billy. "'The Chosen' Makes Big Announcement Amid Streaming Delay, Quest to Bring Show to One Billion People." Faithwire, March 14, 2024. Accessed February 9, 2025. https://www.faithwire.com/2024/03/14/the-chosen-makes-big-announcement-amid-streaming-delay-quest-to-bring-show-to-one-billion-people/.

Hallowell, "'The Chosen' Makes Big Announcement."

Hallowell, "'The Chosen' Makes Big Announcement."

Prison Fellowship. "Overview and Factsheets." Prison Fellowship. Accessed February 9, 2025. https://www.prisonfellowship.org/resources/media-information/overview-and-factsheets/.

Quinn, Alyson R. "Watergate: The Glorious Defeat of Chuck Colson." Prison Fellowship, April 16, 2020. Accessed February 9, 2025. https://www.prisonfellowship.org/story/watergate-the-glorious-defeat-of-chuck-colson/.

Quinn, "Watergate: The Glorious Defeat of Chuck Colson."

Quinn, "Watergate: The Glorious Defeat of Chuck Colson."

Quinn, "Watergate: The Glorious Defeat of Chuck Colson."

GotQuestions.org. "Who Was King Jehoshaphat in the Bible?" GotQuestions.org. Accessed February 9, 2025. https://www.gotquestions.org/King-Jehoshaphat.html.

Power Evangelism

Merriam-Webster. "Miracle." Merriam-Webster.com Dictionary. Accessed February 9, 2025. https://www.merriam-webster.com/dictionary/miracle.

The Holy Bible, New International Version. Grand Rapids: Zondervan, 2011.

Smith Wigglesworth. "Smith Wigglesworth: The Apostle of Faith." Accessed February 9, 2025. https://smithwigglesworth.com/.

Frodsham, Stanley Howard. Smith Wigglesworth: Apostle of Faith. Springfield, MO: Gospel Publishing House, 1948.

Frodsham, Smith Wigglesworth: Apostle of Faith.

Frodsham, Smith Wigglesworth: Apostle of Faith.

Prophetic Evangelism

"Prophetic Evangelism." Premier Christianity, accessed February 9, 2025. https://www.premierchristianity.com/home/prophetic-evangelism/1560.article.

"Prophetic Evangelism."

GotQuestions.org. "What Is the Meaning of the Valley of Dry Bones in Ezekiel 37?" GotQuestions.org. Accessed February 9, 2025. https://www.gotquestions.org/valley-dry-bones.html.

Conclusion: The End Time Mystery of Evangelism

None

www.ingramcontent.com/pod-product-compliance
Lightning Source LLC
Chambersburg PA
CBHW070845120626
46556CB00002B/886